The Combatant

PETER LANG
PROMPT

PETER LANG
New York • Berlin • Brussels • Lausanne • Oxford

Carlos Antonio Aguirre Rojas

The Combatant

A Che Guevara Enigma

PETER LANG

New York • Berlin • Brussels • Lausanne • Oxford

Library of Congress Cataloging-in-Publication Data

Names: Aguirre Rojas, Carlos Antonio, author.
Title: The combatant: a Che Guevara enigma / Carlos Antonio Aguirre Rojas.
Other titles: Pesquisa sobre el Che Guevara. English.
Description: English edition. | New York: Peter Lang, [2023]
Identifiers: LCCN 2022057582 (print) | LCCN 2022057583 (ebook) |
ISBN 9781636670874 (hardback) | ISBN 9781636670850 (ebook) |
ISBN 9781636670867 (epub)
Subjects: LCSH: Guevara, Che, 1928–1967—Authorship. | Runa, Ojarikuj.
Bolivia, análisis de una situación—Authorship. | Bolivia—Politics
and government—1952–1982.
Classification: LCC F2849.22.G85 A5613 2023 (print) | LCC F2849.22.G85
(ebook) | DDC 984.05/2—dc23/eng/20221130
LC record available at https://lccn.loc.gov/2022057582
LC ebook record available at https://lccn.loc.gov/2022057583
DOI 10.3726/b20548

Bibliographic information published by **Die Deutsche Nationalbibliothek**.
Die Deutsche Nationalbibliothek lists this publication in the "Deutsche
Nationalbibliografie"; detailed bibliographic data are available
on the Internet at http://dnb.d-nb.de/.

This publication has been peer reviewed and meets
the highest quality standards for content and production.

© 2023 Peter Lang Publishing, Inc., New York
80 Broad Street, 5th floor, New York, NY 10004
www.peterlang.com

Table of Contents

Prologue to the English Edition ix
List of Abbreviations xix

The Combatant: A Che Guevara Enigma 1
 Truths, Lies, and Historical Conjectures 1
 A Text in Search of Its Author 4
 Just How Anonymous Can a Pseudonym Be? 10
 A Pseudonym in Search of Its Creator 19
 Leads and Clues on a Celebrated Anonymous Someone 32
 The Contingent Motivations of the Celebrated Anonymous
 Someone 44
 Nicknames and Pseudonyms, Collective Authors and
 Anonymous Authors 51

Appendix 59
Bolivia: Analysis of One Situation 59

For Carlo Ginzburg, in testimony of a very special affection and a profound friendship.

Prologue to the English Edition

"In this preface we will anticipate only the measure of our heresy; let us take the time and space necessary to argue it at length."

Ernesto "Che" Guevara, "La necesidad de este libro," in *Apuntes Críticos a la Economía Política*, circa 1965–1966

In the social sciences, any serious and long-term research on a specific topic is always replete with vanishing points. An important part of the research's central argument, a vanishing point is a concrete problem which at a given moment and under particular circumstances may become independent from that general argument. Becoming more and more complex, the vanishing point transforms into a new line of argument, different and autonomous from the one it sprang from.

Such is the case of the book the reader now holds in their hands. It was some years ago now that I first undertook the project of writing an intellectual anti-biography of Che Guevara. This anti-biography would for the first time be capable of recuperating Che's dimensions (not yet seriously studied or analyzed) as a critical Marxist theorist of real *global* significance. Since then, my research has found its way down multiple far-ranging paths which encompass world history during the long twentieth century and the general history of Latin America in the same century, as well as the particular histories of the revolutionary movements and organizations of all of Latin America during that era.

These vast horizons progressively delimit the different contexts that frame and partly explain both the personal odyssey of Ernesto Guevara de la Serna and his rich and complex intellectual journey. They clearly demonstrate the enormous intellectual stature which made Che the most important Latin American Marxist of the second half of the twentieth century, as well as one of the three most important Marxists in the world during the same period, alongside Frantz Fanon (the theorist of the Algerian and African revolutions) and Mao Zedong (the theorist of the Chinese, Asian, and world revolutions).

Conceptualized from these broad frameworks of true global history, our research on the theoretical, analytical, reflective, and intellectual dimensions of Ernesto "Che" Guevara has over the course of its evolution encountered many such vanishing points. Among these vanishing points is the issue of Che's participation in the "long Cuban 1968," that is, in the Cuban manifestation of the World Cultural Revolution of 1968. Like the "specter of communism," this revolution traversed literally the entire world, appearing in France and in Argentina, in the United States and in Japan, in Italy and in China, in Germany and Mexico and of course in Cuba itself, where the Cuban 1968 had the peculiarity of profoundly fusing with the overarching process of the entire Cuban social revolution.

Another vanishing point has been the much-debated problem of Che's position toward the famous Sino-Soviet polemic and the resulting question of whether he was a Maoist, pro-China, anti-Soviet, or none of these, and why then he has been sometimes accused and other times exalted for his positions of clear sympathy toward Mao Zedong and the Chinese Revolution. There is also the vanishing point of why he made his likewise-explicit criticisms of the model of building socialism in the Soviet Union and Eastern Europe.

To these various vanishing points we can add the particular enigma analyzed in this book: Che's possible authorship of a brilliant article published in the sixth issue of the Cuban journal *Pensamiento Crítico* in June 1967, alongside an important manifesto by the Army of National Liberation of Bolivia (ELN). In addition to presenting an observant and profound analysis of Bolivia in 1967, this article, entitled "Bolivia: Análisis de una situación" (Bolivia: Analysis of a Situation), explains the reasons behind, justifications for, and main perspectives of the ELN at the very moment in which this group was sending its combatants against the Bolivian Army and government and in which it was beginning its project of establishing itself in Bolivia.

In reviewing the complete collection of *Pensamiento Crítico*—which beyond a doubt remains the best social sciences journal ever published in revolutionary Cuba—and discovering within it the exceptional article referenced above, a question arose: could the author of that article be Che Guevara himself? This possibility was supported both by elements of the particular context in which the essay was published as well by the positions it advances, in addition to very specific stylistic features of the essay itself. Initially a simple footnote on the curious and still conjectural possibility that this article may have come from Che's own pen, this question later became a brief explanation, some paragraphs long, within the text of the main writing (which currently remains in progress).

But as tends to happen, as the research delved more deeply into the issue of the "Bolivian chapter" of Che's intellectual anti-biography, it became evident that, on one hand, this article had much greater general relevance and significance. If Che's proposed authorship was true, this essay would be the only general and systematic theoretical reflection on why Che chose Bolivia as his initial theater of operations for the project of propelling the Pan-Latin American continental revolution. On the other hand, if Che was the author of the article, this would represent many more analytical implications and consequences than seemed at first glance. But it also became evident that a serious and rigorous inquiry into this question largely overflowed the general line of argument of the abovementioned intellectual anti-biography. It therefore merited a different, specific labor of investigation in terms of the more general research.

It was this double perception of the text's greater relevance and its various fundamental implications, as well as the overflow of general reasoning it implied, that lead to the decision of continuing on to a more detailed investigation surrounding this singular clue of the article on Bolivia signed under and original and not-at-all-casual pseudonym of Ojarikuj Runa, a name which in the Quechua language simply means "combatant." This, briefly summarized, is the origin of *The Combatant: A Che Guevara Enigma*.

* * *

After reading this book, the reader will decide if the hypothesis proposed here is convincing or not. Whatever their impression, it is important to note now that in this book we have limited ourselves only to reviewing the feasibility of this hypothesis, which we do by weighing the reasons for and against it and also by playing with counter-factual reasoning. In other words, we have suggested other possible authors for the article who are not Che Guevara but who fulfill conditions necessary to claim authorship. This is intended to test how probable it is that each of these candidates might be the real writer concealed behind the pseudonym of Ojarikuj Runa, the combatant. We have discarded each candidate, one after the other, for different reasons which we present over the course of the argument we develop here.

Furthermore, in our attempt to "demonstrate" we have not limited ourselves to a single kind of argument but rather to three different kinds of reasoning. First are the elements that correspond to the *context* in which "Bolivia: Analysis of a Situation" was published. Later come the essay's *ideas*, the theoretical content of its forceful theses. Finally, we use the *stylistic* dimension of the text, its literary form of presentation. Based on the three genres of arguments analyzed, we always reach the same conclusion: the most likely author of "Bolivia: Analysis of a Situation" is Che Guevara. However, the primary objective of this book was first to show and then to prove Che's authorship of the essay, and we have not elaborated here upon the main implications and consequences which stem from this hypothesis should it prove to be correct.

This book was published in 2021 in Mexico and Argentina, and there has already been a reviewer who has asserted that even if we accept that the hypothesis is true and Che Guevara is the author of "Bolivia: Analysis of a Situation," this fact is neither relevant nor meaningful. Even if this thesis is true, he says, it represents no substantial change for our analyses, our way of understanding and explaining the complex figure who Che was.

This assertion, in our opinion, is completely mistaken. It only confirms once again the inadequacy which continues to characterize the general perception and current understanding of Che Guevara despite the dozens of biographies which have been written about him, as well the hundreds of articles on different aspects of his life and work. It is appropriate, then, that in this brief prologue we venture to "anticipate only the measure of our heresy," to return to Che's own phrase, explicitly mentioning some of the possible consequences that may derive from our authorial hypothesis being true and clarifying that these derivations may, for example, help to refute certain cliches regarding Che's thought and action which are mistaken no matter how tenaciously they continue to be repeated. Likewise, these derivations may also serve to discover elements of Che's life and work which have been ignored or undervalued until now. We briefly mention only some of these here, as their broader treatment will form part of the issues that will be addressed in detail in the intellectual anti-biography of Che mentioned above, which is still under development.

If, then, we carefully read "Bolivia: Analysis of a Situation" and agree that its author is Che Guevara, this text once again clearly demonstrates the complex and heightened theoretical caliber which Che had achieved by 1967. It was this stature as a theorist that allowed him to create this profound and complete analysis of the Bolivia of his time, where he decided (almost at the last minute but at the same time on a broad, well-justified basis) to establish the "mother guerrilla column" from which different guerrilla movements would spring to fight in the rest of Latin America. This profound analysis incorporates an understanding which is simultaneously historical, economic, sociological, political, and cultural. In addition to supplying the keys for explaining the essential structures of the Bolivian nation in the 1970s, the text is also able to demonstrate the specific articulation of all those dimensions a way that assembles a truly comprehensive analysis of Bolivia in the most astute and adequate style of the primary lessons of Marx regarding the analysis of any type of reality, which assert that any analysis must always be developed from the point of view of the totality.

It bears emphasizing that in the history of the social sciences and critical thought of the last 50 years, very few social theorists, Marxist or otherwise, have been capable of developing this type of truly complete analysis of the issue or reality they study. Very few have been capable of developing an analysis that incorporates the dimensions which we have noted in "Bolivia: Analysis of a Situation," an analysis which does not simply enunciate and tally up these dimensions but shows their complex articulation and the way that all of these, as a combined totality in movement, allow us to rationally and intelligently take stock of the particular problem we are investigating and attempting to explain.

And while Guevara builds that critical, totalizing, and articulated vision of Bolivia in 1967 in synchronous terms, he also presents, in diachronic terms, the historical elements which over the course of their complex evolution led to the singular situation that he analyzes. He furthermore connects immediate causes with medium-term junctural evolutions and long-term processes that link the military dictatorship of René Barrientos to the important but failed Bolivian Revolution of 1952 and the role of the Revolutionary Nationalist Movement (MNR) in leading that revolution to its failure, as well as to the single-product character of the Bolivian economy—centered entirely around the production of tin—and with the secular survival of indigenous communitarian structures in the Bolivian countryside, among many other elements.

In this perceptive article, Che Guevara therefore also contributes a brilliant example of Lenin's "concrete analysis of a concrete situation." We should not forget that while this kind of analysis is always easy to propose, it is truly difficult to achieve, and it is one that very few authors, have been able to develop in the last century and a half, especially in the complex and specific terms set out by Lenin.

Executing this dense, totalizing, and concrete historical analysis of the Bolivia in which he was fighting and organizing the struggle, Che shows a trace of his complex personality which has not yet been adequately appraised by the vast majority of his biographers or the analysts of his life and especially his work. That trace is his constant, alert, and profound reflective activity, which always lead him to seriously and deeply investigate the context or task he faced at any given moment. When Che wanted to learn about Latin America, for example, he read about and researched the region. When he made the revolution in Cuba in 1957 and 1958, he reflected upon and theorized the lessons of his own action, which he would later set out in the brilliant reflection that is his book *Guerrilla Warfare*.

The same was true when he directed Cuba's process of industrialization, and more generally the process of building a specifically Cuban form of socialism, around which he facilitated a titanic intellectual debate of the highest level which saw the participation of the world's most important contemporary Marxist economists in 1963 and 1964. The same was true when Che undertook new radical revolutionary struggles, first in Congo—in preparation for which Che studiously researched the situation of Africa as a whole—and later in Bolivia, where Che resumed and deepened his constant research on the Latin American context and on Bolivia itself, as we observe in the article which is the subject of this book.

For this reason, "Bolivia: Analysis of a Situation" is immediately striking for its resemblance to other texts by Che, such as his "La Influencia de la Revolución Cubana en América Latina" (The Influence of the Cuban Revolution in Latin America); "Conferencia en el Ministerio de Industria" (Conference at the Ministry of Industry), from March 1965; and his celebrated "Message to the Tricontinental," whose title Che actually intended to be "The Slogan Is: Create Two, Three… Many Vietnams." The first text is a critical and profound analysis of Latin America in 1962; the second is a complete and rigorous overview of the entire African continent in 1965; and the third is a well-grounded and critical examination of the most important revolutionary struggles which were developing across the planet in 1966 and 1967. These diverse analytical projects—to which, in our opinion, we must add the creative and trenchant analysis of the Bolivian situation in 1967—demonstrate that Che would first carry out a careful diagnosis of each subject that caught his interest or of a context in which he planned to act and would then organize his specific practical and political action on the solid theoretical and analytical basis he had already formulated.

Later, he would perform a clear movement of return: at the same time at which Che acted or would implement a series of practical measures on an issue or process or problem, he would continue to reflect on it in order to keep perfecting his own analytical comprehension and theoretical explanations of the practical action and concrete activities he undertook.

If Che is indeed the author of the essay signed under the name Ojarikuj Runa, this would illustrate the sophisticated degree of understanding which he had of Bolivia, the country where he finally decided to establish the initial structure of his mother guerrilla column, his "international school for Latin American guerrillas." After discarding Peru and on the basis of his solid and far-ranging knowledge of its conditions, it was Bolivia that Che chose for this daring initiative. Knowing this gives us a well-founded basis upon which to refute the absurd criticisms that various authors have made of Che over more than 50 years, asserting that Che did not know where he would be going to fight, or even that it was not him who chose Bolivia, or that the decision was last minute and circumstantial, made half at random and half-blindly. Confronted with the depth and rigor of the analysis contained in "Bolivia: Analysis of a Situation," these ridiculous criticisms collapse under the weight of their vacuousness and unsustainability.

Reading the text on Bolivia, however, shows that Che had perfectly detailed knowledge of the country's particular juncture prior to the military coup of November 1964 and of its situation at the end of 1966. The latter situation was marked by an increasingly unpopular military dictatorship and by a highly politicized population which had directly created the popular revolution of 1952, defeating the Bolivian Army in the cities and the countryside. The Bolivian people had furthermore already extrapolated the lessons of the limits and final failure of the lukewarm and accommodationist government lead by the MNR, as well as of this party itself. This politicized and rebellious people included a well-organized and powerful working class with its own workers' militias; a critical and participative professional middle class and student population; and mass segments of the peasantry and city dwellers who were vigilant and willing to support genuine mass movements. In other words, the Bolivia described by the article in question was experiencing a real pre-revolutionary situation. It failed to become a true social revolution only because it lacked time to mature as a result of the tragically brief life of the ELN's guerrilla campaign, which was unable to survive its first year of existence.

The text not only reveals Che's vast knowledge of Bolivia in general but also his significant understanding of its different regions, which explains his choice of Ñancahuazú as the initial site of the mother guerrilla column instead of Upper Beni or the Chaparé. The primary justifications for this choice are clearly laid out in the subsection of the essay titled "The Theater of Operations" and once again refute Che's critics who affirm that his choice of southern Bolivia was based on purely coincidental reasons or on simple ignorance.

The truth, just as "Bolivia: Analysis of a Situation" convincingly argues, is that the selected region was entirely strategic; it was close, for example, to the principal Bolivian oilfield of the time and was connected by railroad to Brazil and Argentina. Furthermore, in what was a highly conscious choice on Che's part, the area was relatively sparsely populated by a small population of peasants. This was favorable for the initial work of that guerrilla mother column, the Latin American school of guerrillas, which in Che's original plan was not immediately supposed to seek out combat with its enemies. Instead, the plan was to clandestinely train guerrillas from across Latin America for several years before bursting onto the public stage as a specifically *Bolivian* guerrilla movement and directly confronting the Bolivian government and state such as they existed at the time. This explains the fact that there were various Peruvians in the ELN and that, before being forced to fight the Bolivian Army, Che had attempted to recruit guerrillas from various left-wing groups in Argentina, in addition to maintaining contact with the Chilean Army of National Liberation as well as various armed groups in Brazil, among others.

This essay also demonstrates Che's ability to adapt nimbly to changing circumstances. In his original plan, the mother guerrilla column would be established in southern Bolivia and there discretely mature over the course of several years, training guerrillas from across Latin America who would later organize their own guerrilla movements in their native countries or join struggles already underway there. Only later, in a second phase, would the mother guerrilla column be able to transform itself into a specifically Bolivian guerrilla movement, launching open guerrilla war in Bolivia itself. It is clear, however, that Che had foreseen that this ideal plan could change radically at any time, initiating the second phase earlier than scheduled and overlapping it with the first. This was what eventually came to pass.

But as can be seen in the article to which we have now referred so many times, Che was able to adapt deftly to this new situation, putting that now prematurely Bolivian guerrilla movement into action and directly confronting the Army and government of Bolivia while leaving his original plan temporarily suspended but not abandoned. It was Che's opinion that the guerrilla mother column could be a process that it was possible to resume organically, either when power had already been taken in Bolivia or, failing that, at least when that guerrilla movement was solidly established in the country and in control of territory that would allow it to develop and fluidly maintain that guerrilla-school-*cum*-mother-guerrilla-column. Because from the time of his arrival in Bolivia in November 1966 to his cowardly murder in October 1967, Che always maintained his general project, which was not simply to make the revolution in Bolivia or Peru or even his native Argentina, but to organize, from a given site in South America, the *Latin American-scale* project of creating a second or third Vietnam, just as he emphatically affirms in his celebrated "Message to the Tricontinental."

In our opinion, this ambitious and profound project of cultivating a Vietnam of Latin American dimensions is completely consistent with the Quechua pseudonym that Che uses to sign his essay on Bolivia, which clearly, radically, and not by coincidence means "combatant." This is one more lesson we take from Che's authorship of this essay: that in terms of his place in the world and his central task in the era in which he lived, Che always perceived himself as a radical and anti-capitalist combatant. Now, it falls to the reader to judge the truth or falsehood of the hypothesis set out in the pages of this book.

Carlos Antonio Aguirre Rojas
August 2022

List of Abbreviations

COB	Confederación Obrera Boliviana
COMIBOL	Corporación Minera Boliviana
EGP	Ejército Guerrillero del Pueblo (Argentina)
ELN	Ejército de Liberación Nacional de Bolivia
FRB	Frente de la Revolución Boliviana
FSTB	Federación Sindical de Trabajadores de Bolivia
MPC	Movimiento Popular Cristiano
MNR	Movimiento Nacionalista Revolucionario
PCB	Partido Comunista de Bolivia
PIR	Partido de Izquierda Revolucionario
PRIN	Partido Revolucionario de la Izquierda Nacionalista
YPFB	Yacimientos Petrolíferos Fiscales Bolivianos

The Combatant: A Che Guevara Enigma

"Each rifle wielded by a guerrilla holds the dawn that will illuminate our land. [...] we can laugh at death, because we know that of that blood will be born our country, a different country [...]"
Ojarikuj Runa, "Bolivia: Análisis de una situación," June 1967

Truths, Lies, and Historical Conjectures

As the best traditions and foremost authors of truly *critical* history have always shown us—from Karl Marx to Carlo Ginzburg, with Walter Benjamin, Marc Bloch, Mikhail Bakhtin, Fernand Braudel, Norbert Elias, Michel Foucault, Bolívar Echeverría, Edward Palmer Thompson, and Immanuel Wallerstein (among others) in between—the basic objective of a historian's work is to discover, reconstruct, and coherently explain different historical truths on a well-grounded basis. These truths correspond to the different issues and problems which, taking up the tools and perspectives of the muse Clio, we decide to address in our particular research.[1]

This endless search is central to historical truth; among many other elements and contrary to irrational and absurd postmodernist approaches to history, it clearly distinguishes the work of historians from that of novelists, writers, and artists in general. Far from constructing simple narrative accounts or mere more-or-less-successful descriptions of particular events, truly critical historians seek to reconstruct *real, true* facts, events, and processes, always providing the relevant proof which *shows* the veracity of these historical facts and processes. Moreover, critical historians accompany this proof with interpretive models, astute hypotheses, and comprehensive frameworks of these historical incidents and realities.

Genuinely critical history distances itself both from tedious positivist descriptions (nothing but a "collection of dead facts," as Marx correctly described them in *The German Ideology*) and new iterations of the contemporary irrationality represented by post-modern approaches to history, which reduce history to vulgar "fiction stories with pretensions to the truth." This, however, does not sweep away the fact that, when faced with sources and historical testimony, the critical historian must also confront the complex and multifaceted dialectic between truth and lies—between what is true and what is false—but also the dialectic between truth and fiction; or between truth and the imaginary; or between certain truth and possible, probable, or plausible truths, when these truths are not merely believable, realistic, or uncertain.

Both clear, conclusive truth and total, unquestionable certainty regarding a specific historical or social reality are opposed not only by lies or historical falsehood or by complete uncertainty but rather by a complex and varied, gradual and progressive *range* of truth. Between both extremes—that of historical truth and that of complete falsity of the evidence—lie the very plausible, the plausible, the very probable,

---

1   On these traditions and the foremost authors of genuinely *critical* history, cf. Carlos Antonio Aguirre Rojas, *Pensadores Críticos del "Largo" Siglo XX. Ensayos de Biografía Intelectual*, Universidad Pública de El Alto, El Alto, Bolivia, 2018; and *Lessons in Critical Theory: Marx, Benjamin, Braudel, Bakhtin, Thompson, Ginzburg and Wallerstein*, Peter Lang, New York, 2020.

the probable, the very possible, the possible, the somewhat uncertain, the uncertain, the indefinite, and the extremely uncertain, among many other possible variants.[2]

As a part of history, conclusive and unquestionable historical truths represent only *one part* of what a historian can recover and reconstruct based on the testimonies and sources accessible to them. Consequently, the cultivation of the office governed by the muse Clio is frequently obliged to resort to the resource of creating justified *historical conjecture*; in order words, plausible hypotheses which are as realistic as possible in order to justifiably, rationally, and intelligently explain the matter being researched.

In assuming that absolute truth does *not* exist and that all truths are *relative*, historical conjectures lead us not toward the irrationalist swamp of absurd post-modern approaches but instead to the astute recognition that historical truth is built and obtained *progressively*. In the process of constantly refining and perfecting these historical truths, it is possible (and even common) to abandon certain "truths" or "certainties" which were once believed to be settled or consecrated. It is also possible to reassess, in enormously varying ways, an explanation for or interpretive model of a particular historical dimension which we believed to be established and immovable, or to partially or entirely revise the approach, viewpoint, or outlook previously adopted to address a given specific historical situation or process.

Because if historical truth is not forthcoming and resists showing itself even after a historian has studied it meticulously and adequately, then it becomes not only valid and possible but even necessary and legitimate to turn to the creation of historical conjectures. Based on careful analysis—of context, of historical antecedents, of the processes directly linked to these antecedents, and of the causes and consequences of the same—conjecture allows us to propose plausible and

---

2   Regarding this complex range of the statute of historical truth and untruth, cf. Carlo Ginzburg, *Relaciones de Fuerza: Historia, Retórica, Prueba* (particularly Chapter 1, "Aristóteles y la Historia, Una Vez Más"), Contrahistorias, Mexico, 2018 and *El Hilo y las Huellas: Lo Verdadero, Lo Falso, Lo Ficticio*, Fondo de Cultura Económica, Buenos Aires, 2010.

justified hypotheses of that sometimes-rebellious and uncertain historical truth for which we search.

It is precisely such a set of justified historical conjectures that we
wish to set out now for scrutiny and consideration by the truly critical
workers of Clio's rich and lively workshop as well as the range of read-
ers of this essay.

A Text in Search of Its Author

Reviewing the complete collection of the Cuban journal *Pensamiento
Crítico*—which was beyond a doubt *Cuba's most important journal of social
sciences* during the global Cultural Revolution of 1968—we find a journal which clearly places itself among the most *radical and anti-capitalist*
positions on the overall spectrum of the then-lively and highly active
Cuban Revolution. Not only this: in its pages, *Pensamiento Critico*
attempts to gather the different contemporary positions surrounding
the primary theoretical, political, philosophical, and historical debates
on the general revolutionary praxis of its time.[3]

As one of the conspicuous expressions of the exceptional "Cuban
1968" (and indeed, of that global Cultural Revolution which made itself
present on that rebel Caribbean island, as it did all over the world)
Pensamiento Crítico served a double function. First, it was an exceptional
intellectual manifestation of the Cuban Revolution itself. Second, it was
a specifically Cuban product of the radical cultural rupture brought on
by the movements of 1968 across the world. Because something that
distinguishes that Cuban 1968 from other similar movements is that, in
addition to its respectable duration of more than a decade (comparable to the long Italian 1968 and the long 1968 of the Chinese Cultural
Revolution) is the fact that in Cuba, the Cultural Revolution of 1968 and
the radical social revolution of all of Cuban society fused into a single process and created a cultural transformation of such dimensions
that between 1959 and 1971 it transformed Cuba into the real *cultural*

---

3   The complete *Pensamiento Crítico* collection can be consulted online on the web-
     site of the Centro de Documentación e Investigación de la Cultura de Izquierda
     (CEDEMI): http://cedinci.org.

vanguard front of the entire Latin American world in those years of the seventh *historical*, not chronological, decade of the past century.[4]

For this reason, *Pensamiento Crítico* was simultaneously an advanced, exceptional journal of social science and a potent intellectual lever for driving —within Cuba— the profound process of total, truly anti-capitalist and revolutionary transformations, and for driving in Latin America the clear project of continentalizing the radical socialist and anti-capitalist revolution against both Latin American and world capitalism as well as US imperialism. This accounts for the fact that in its various issues, rich and penetrating theoretical texts of the most advanced Marxist debates of the period coexist, combine, and complement each other. Texts authored by thinkers like Theodore Adorno, Paul Baran, Georg Lukacs, Rudi Dutschke, Karl Korsch, Henri Lefebvre, and Ernesto "Che" Guevara appear alongside articles, essays, and interviews on the struggles then underway in Peru, Guatemala, Venezuela, and Bolivia, as well as in Rwanda, Portuguese Guinea, the United States, Cambodia, and Vietnam.[5]

The journal was groundbreaking and exceptional in many senses, comparable to what the Mexican journal *Cuadernos Políticos* would be in the 1970s and 1980s. *Pensamiento Crítico* was only published from 1961 to 1971, on an astonishing monthly basis with a likewise impressive print

4   On the general characterization of 1968, cf. *La Revolución Cultural Mundial de 1968*, Desde Abajo, Bogota, 2018, which includes texts by Fernand Braudel, Immanuel Wallerstein, and Carlos Antonio Aguirre Rojas, among others. On the long Italian 1968, cf. Nanni Balestrini and Primo Moroni, *L'orda d'oro 1968–1977*, Feltrinelli, Milan, 2003; on 1968 in China, cf. K. H. Fan *La Revolución Cultural China*, Ediciones Era, Mexico, 1975. On the singular, profound Cuban 1968 and its important reach in all of Latin America, cf. *Mirar a los 60: Antología Cultural de una Década*, Museo Nacional de Bellas Artes, Havana, 2004; Graziella Pogolotti, *Polémicas Culturales de los 60*, Letras Cubanas, Havana, 2006; and Jorge Fornet, *El 71: Anatomía de una crisis*, Letras Cubanas, Havana, 2014.
5   Regarding the singular profile of *Pensamiento Crítico*, Fernando Martínez Heredia, its only director, affirms: "How could we make Cuban thought ideal for pushing the Revolution forward, for forcing it to examine itself, self-criticize, renew itself, change itself, be better? And at the same time, how to multiply its forces, which were so small compared to the forces of Imperialism or world capitalism [...]? These are the needs and challenges that gave birth to *Pensamiento Crítico*." In Fernando Martínez Heredia, "A 40 años de *Pensamiento Crítico*," in *Crítica y Emancipación*, Vol. 1, No. 1, June 2008, p. 241.

run of 15,000 copies which were distributed across Cuba. Significantly, these were also distributed throughout Latin America in order to irradiate Cuba's culture and revolution on a Latin American scale, thus confirming Fernand Braudel's astute 1965 thesis that "the Cuban Revolution continues to be the burning bonfire and the dividing line of Latin America's destinies."[6]

Alongside that world-class intellectual, this exceptional Cuban journal (an offspring of the likewise extraordinary process of the Cuban 1968) also radically assumed the task of turning itself into an authentic sounding board of the principal contemporary revolutionary movements across the world, especially those of Latin America. This explains the fact that its first issue is comprised of four lengthy texts, each written by revolutionary militants of the guerrilla movements then active in Colombia, Venezuela, Peru, and Guatemala. Two of these four texts were published *not* under the real names of their authors but under pseudonyms. For this reason, Fernando Martínez Heredia, *Pensamiento Crítico*'s director for its entire brief existence, has clearly stated that "the issue of the revolutionary movements was one of the journal's primary lines. The first three issues were dedicated to the revolutionary movements of Latin America, Africa, and Asia."[7] Likewise, this explains the fact that of the 377 authors who contributed to the journal, the author most published was Che Guevara, who published 35 articles in *Pensamiento Crítico* and even had two entire issues dedicated to him. Beyond a doubt, this was due to the explicit sympathy the journal had for Guevara's radical positions, and later for his tragic and heroic death in Bolivia.

If within Cuba itself *Pensamiento Crítico* represented one of the most radically *anti-capitalist* intellectual expressions of the overall spectrum

---

6   Cf. Fernand Braudel, *Las civilizaciones actuales*, Editorial Tecnos, Madrid, 1978, p. 393. It is possible that this idea of Braudel's was born out of reading Jean-Paul Sartre's articles in the French journal *L'Express*, later compiled as Sartre's book *Huracán sobre el Azúcar*, Ediciones Uruguay, Montevideo, 1961.

7   On the Fernando Martínez Heredia quote included in this paragraph, cf. "A 40 años de *Pensamiento Crítico*," op. cit., p. 243. On the 377 authors and Che's 35 articles published in the journal, cf. Vilma N. Ponce Suárez, "Una mirada métrica a la revista *Pensamiento Crítico*," in the journal *Bibliotecas: Annales de Investigación*, No. 3, January-December 2007.

of the Cuban Revolution, this is clearly expressed in some of its many Editorials and several of its comments on particular published articles, in which it is clear that the journal openly defends the path of armed struggle and the method of guerrilla war as legitimate and sometimes even essential means of winning true, radical social emancipation for the oppressed peoples of the world.

For this reason, glossing a published text which criticizes Peruvian guerrillas, the journal vindicates the experiences of guerrilla movements in Peru to conclude by affirming that "what is necessary is to analyze, from revolutionary positions and with revolutionary intentions, the experiences of the armed struggle." On another occasion, criticizing the reformist and official Lefts of the world, generally located within the pro-Soviet Communist Parties of the world at the time, the journal states that "the traditional left, out of so much respect for the system's structures—economic, social, cultural and political—had become one more mechanism of this [system] and even, to a not-inconsiderable degree, one of its most important safety valves." This was precisely what the Cultural Revolution of 1968 had come to demonstrate and denounce in the eyes of the entire world.[8]

This clear posture of sympathy toward guerilla warfare and the armed struggle, which was very close to the positions of Che Guevara, also then explains why the journal gladly and repeatedly published texts by authors including Carlos Marighella (who openly defended the path of armed struggle and urban guerrilla war in Brazil) and the National Liberation Army of Bolivia (ELN), who likewise were partisans of the guerrilla struggle in Bolivia and across Latin America. It also explains the entire issues dedicated to the heroic struggle of the Vietnamese people against the United States, the Arab-Israeli war, the various struggles spread out across Africa, and the complex situation of the struggles and movements of Guatemala and Brazil.

---

8   The first quote of this paragraph is the editorial Comment which opens Américo Pumaruna's (pseudonym of the Peruvian Ricardo Letts Colmenaro) article "Perú: revolución, insurrección, guerrillas," in issue 1 of *Pensamiento Crítico*, p. 76. The second is taken from the Editorial of the journal's double issue (25–26), which was dedicated to the celebrated French May of 1968.

Based on these specific profiles of this Cuban journal, it is not at all strange that in its sixth issue, published in July 1967, we find a profound and incisive article titled "Bolivia: Análisis de una situación" (Bolivia: Analysis of a Situation), which brilliantly and penetratingly describes the social, economic, cultural, and political situation which Bolivia was then experiencing, as well as the role which the ELN, which had only recently entered the public eye, had begun to play in Bolivia a few months earlier. Thus, in beginning to closely study this text, we realize that it attempts to explain and justify the existence and actions of the ELN after its existence was first made public following the military actions of March 23, 1967. Furthermore, alongside that explanation of the reasons for its existence, the text also seeks to broadly disseminate—throughout Cuba and Latin America—the location, size, extensiveness, social base, short-, medium-, and long-term objectives, and specific impact of the ELN's struggle within Bolivia itself and in Latin America generally.[9]

Reading this profound and intelligent analysis of the Bolivian situation in 1967—which masterfully describes and criticizes the Revolution of 1952 and its limited and failed agrarian reform, as well as its deformed and unfortunate drift which ended in the military coup d'état of 1964—we recall that the guerrilla movement established by the ELN was planned and later organized, built, and always led by Che Guevara. Indeed, at the very moment of this article's publication, Che was fighting in the mountains and jungles of southern Bolivia. In doing so, he was attempting to establish a second or third "Vietnam" on Latin American soil which would make it possible to spread the struggle from Bolivia toward Peru, Chile, Brazil, Argentina, Paraguay, etc., continentalizing the project of the Cuban Revolution and in this way confronting oppressive US imperialism in a broader, more effective manner.[10]

---

9 See the article referenced, Ojarikuj Runa, "Bolivia: Análisis de una situación," in *Pensamiento Crítico*, No. 6, July 1967, pp. 204–220 This text is also included as the Appendix of this book.

10 On the clearly *continental* scope of Che's guerrilla campaign in Bolivia, which Che *explicitly* declared on various occasions, e.g., in his journal of that struggle, cf. Ernesto Guevara, "Diario de Campaña," in *El Che en Bolivia: Documentos y Testimonios*, Vol. I, La Razón, La Paz, 2005, pp. 54 (December 31, 1966 entry), 72 (February 14, 1967 entry) and 98 (April 13, 1967 entry), as well as "Mensaje a los pueblos del mundo a través de la Tricontinental," in *Obras Escogidas: 1957–1967*, Vol. II, Editorial de

However, in July 1967, when "Bolivia: Analysis of a Situation" was published, the fact that Che was present in Bolivia and leading the ELN was *not* public knowledge, much less confirmed. On the other hand, the ELN had already been compelled to confront and battle the Bolivian Army, which in turn made it strategically important to spread the news not only of the ELN itself but of its objectives, struggle, and social impact, as well as the larger meaning of its existence. In disseminating this information throughout Cuba and all of Latin America, the aim was to awaken the sympathy—and, above all, the alert solidarity and militant attention—of all followers and defenders of the Cuban Revolution and all truly anti-capitalist Latin American revolutionaries for this Army of National Liberation, thus increasing its impact in Latin America and its chances of survival, continued action, and future victory.

It should be noted that "Bolivia: Analysis of a Situation" fully meets all these goals and does so in a penetrating, keen, and brilliant manner. This brings us to a logical question: who is the author of this text that has such clear and relevant militant political ends, published at such a strategic moment via the most important Cuban and Latin American theoretical-political social sciences journal of the time? The answer to this question: the author of this exceptional and penetrating essay is Ojarikuj Runa.

So, surprised by the brilliance and perceptiveness of the article and now knowing its authors name, we ask ourselves: What other articles or books might Ojarikuj Runa have written? Where might he have received his academic and political education? What was his political militancy, or his previous ideological trajectory? Trying to answer these questions, we research texts or information on this author that might exist on the internet. We find nothing. Later, we turn to the last page of Issue 6 of *Pensamiento Crítico*, a page titled "The Authors," which always provided a short informative and biographical note on the authors who contributed to each issue of the journal. But coming at last to this page, we find a surprise: Ojarikuj Runa *does not exist.*

Ciencias Sociales, Havana, 2007; and Manuel Piñeiro, *Che Guevara y la Revolución Latinoamericana*, Ocean Sur, Havana, 2006.

Because instead of describing this supposed contributor's biographical information and work, all his author's note tells the reader is that in the Quechua language, Ojarikuj Runa means "combatant." In other words, the author of this brilliant essay on the situation in Bolivia is simply a combatant, which means that Ojarikuj Runa is nothing more than a *pseudonym*.

Just How Anonymous Can a Pseudonym Be?

In contrast to other authors who published texts in *Pensamiento Crítico* under pseudonyms and whose real names were later divulged, it appears that the real name of the author who used the Quechua pseudonym of combatant, Ojarikuj Runa, has never been revealed. Who might this Ojarikuj Runa be, who in July 1967 was capable of laying out such a perceptive and brilliant analysis of the Bolivian juncture and of the legitimacy and relevance of the first public actions of the Army of National Liberation (ELN)? In order to narrow down the universe of the possible answers to this question, we believe in the possibility of following a double strategy, inspired by various lessons in critical methodology contained in the work of Carlo Ginzburg.

The first lesson is that of contrasting various elements, affirmations, and indications contained in the text itself against the extra-textual elements of its specific context, that is, the specific historical realities in which this singular article was developed, written, and finally published. The second is to try to execute an "indiciary reading" of the essay itself. This type of reading simultaneously detects certain stylistic strokes, metaphors or comparisons, and strong theses or explanations and recognizes these as possible "indicias." An indiciary reading uses these elements as clues or points of entry that allow us to access the hidden reality behind the pseudonym; in other words, that let us access the possible identity of the true author of the article in question.[11]

---

11 These two strategies take clear inspiration from the work of Carlo Ginzburg. The first is based on his book *Pesquisa sobre Piero*, Muchnick, Barcelona, 1984, and its complex interplay between the artistic elements of the work of Piero della Francesca and the extra-artistic elements of that work's specific context. The second draws on his celebrated essay "Indicios: Raíces de un paradigma de inferencias indiciales," in

In this sense, an interesting first lead we might detect in the essay at hand is found in an affirmation it makes after describing the Revolutionary Nationalist Movement (MNR). The MNR was the ruling party of Bolivia after the 1952 Revolution, promoting significant social and economic changes, including the nationalization of tin mines and a timid, limited agrarian reform, before later reversing its course and veering increasingly to the right. The MNR gradually delegitimized itself, losing a significant part of the support it had initially enjoyed from the poor and working classes, and eventually ended in the military coup of 1964. It bears noting that the MNR was a highly complex and disjointed amalgamation of groups, positions, sectors, and social classes ranging from certain members of the pro-imperialist, US-aligned bourgeoisie, to radical sections of the working class, peasants, and petit-bourgeoisie.

In light of this, the article affirms that, despite the MNR's betrayal of the people and despite the military coup of 1964, there is "participation of MNR militants in the Army of National Liberation" (p. 212). This affirmation stands in contrast to the well-known fact that the Bolivians who joined the ELN's guerrilla campaign came not from the Bolivian MNR but from either (in their immense majority) the pro-Soviet, traditional Bolivian Communist Party, which they eventually broke with, or from the group led by Moisés Guevara, a mine worker leader who was first active in Oscar Zamora's pro-China Communist Party. Expelled by Zamora's party, Moisés's convictions later drove him to join the ELN alongside several comrades. Why, then, does this essay affirm that the ELN counts former MNR militants among its ranks?

Verifying the biographies and political trajectories of the ELN's 52 members and their party affiliations, we find that of the ELN's 29 Bolivian militants, only one was an MNR member: Jaime Arana Campero, alias Chapaco or Luis. Arana Campero had belonged to the

---

Tentativas, Prohistoria, Rosario, 2004, and on his exceptional book *El queso y los gusanos*, Muchnik, Barcelona, 1991, which show us how we can learn to "read the indicia," in the strict and broad senses, in order to discover certain elements of the truth which are not easily accessible to researchers. Cf. also Carlos Antonio Aguirre Rojas, *Microhistoria Italiana: Claves y Modo de Empleo*, Instituto Cubano de Arte e Industria Cinematográficos; Instituto de Historia de Cuba, Havana, 2018; and "Indicios, lecturas indiciarias, estrategia indiciaria y saberes populares: Una hipótesis sobre los límites de la racionalidad burguesa moderna," in *Contrahistorias*, No. 7, 2006.

MNR in his youth and later joined the ELN, but this was because he had studied in Cuba, *not* because of his earlier militancy in the MNR.[12] This raises two other questions: first, who, in or outside of Bolivia, could have been so informed as to the previous political affiliations of the members of the underground and almost-unknown ELN that they could affirm that some of these members belonged or had belonged to the MNR? Second, if the ELN had only one ex-MNR member, why does the article use the plural "militants" and not the singular "militant"?

The first question presents a possible hypothesis: the author of the article we are scrutinizing might be Haydée Tamara Bunke Bíder, better known as Tania the Guerrillera. Bunke was one of the central figures of the urban support network for Che Guevara's rural guerrilla movement. Her authorship is supported by the fact that she arrived in Bolivia at the end of 1964, on Che's orders, and for two years managed not only to penetrate the highest circles of the Bolivian government and ruling classes but to play a key role in structuring that urban support network, in which she was a central operator. She therefore knew many of those who would later be members of the ELN and was also aware of parts of their political trajectories, affiliations, and memberships in different Bolivian political parties.

However, we must remember that for conspiratorial security reasons, the structure of the ELN's urban network was highly compartmentalized and that information about the pasts and presents of many of its members did not circulate much and was not known by all its members, which limits Tania's possible knowledge on this point. Furthermore, it is known that Tania, despite being a highly intelligent and educated woman (who had studied philosophy and was fluent in various languages) was much more inclined toward practical-political work and direct activity than toward theoretical and intellectual work or writing texts or essays.

---

12 For information on the overall composition of the guerrilla campaign, the number of Bolivians within it, and each one's political and partisan affiliations, cf. "Composición de la Guerrilla" and "Notas Biográficas," both included in *El Che en Bolivia: Documentos y Testimonios*, Vol. I, op. cit, pp. 193–195 and 197–220, respectively.

This particular inclination, which she discussed openly, led her to declare, in the brief autobiography she writes for the Cuban intelligence services, that although she has a very good personal relationship with her brother, "[...] we were always distanced somewhat by our different concerns; his, for science and purely intellectual work, and mine for politics and revolutionary activities." These reasons lead us to think that it would be quite difficult to assume that Tamara Bunke could be the author behind the Quechua pseudonym that means combatant.[13]

The second question might be answered by saying that the text's author is speaking *generically* and therefore using the plural form instead of the singular. But given that there was really only *one* MNR militant—who furthermore had only been active in the MNR in his youth and had joined the ELN *not* because of that first militancy but because of his studies and time spent in revolutionary Cuba—we must search for another explanation for this use of plural instead of singular. This possible alternative explanation does exist, and it is linked to the fact that when "Bolivia: Analysis of a Situation" was written, there was a firm expectation that a significant contingent of MNR members or ex-members would become directly incorporated into the ELN's guerrilla movement.

In April 1967, in Havana, the Cubans interviewed Juan Lechín Oquendo, who had been a union leader in the Bolivian Workers' Confederation (COB) at the time of the 1952 Revolution and was therefore a prominent member of the MNR. Furthermore, Lechín was later Minister for Mines and Vice President of Bolivia, and later served as Ambassador of Bolivia in Italy, a post he held until the military coup of 1964. When the text analyzed here was written, Juan Lechín had just promised the Cubans that he would soon secretly return to Bolivia and upon his return, in addition to making a public statement of support for the ELN, would also send the organization a sizeable contingent of members of his Party so that these could join the guerrilla struggle.

---

13 On the elements of the biography of Haydée Tamara Bunke Bíder noted here and on her work in the Bolivian urban network, cf. Ulises Estrada, *Tania la guerrillera y la epopeya suramericana del Che*, Ocean Press, Havana, 2005. The quote reproduced in this paragraph is included in Annex 1 of that book, "Autobiografia elaborada por el 'Caso Tania,'" page 154.

That party was the Revolutionary Party of the Nationalist Left (PRIN), which Lechín himself had founded with the left-wing segments of the MNR. The Cubans inform Che of this project and begin to prepare the conditions for an eventual personal meeting between Juan Lechín and Che. They also ask Che to later send them a list of information on MNR members who wish to train in the ELN under his leadership.[14] Unfortunately, neither the interview nor the incorporation of the MNR or PRIN members into the ELN will ever happen: Juan Lechín will be arrested in May 1967 while attempting to clandestinely enter Bolivia through its border with Chile and Peru.

Regardless, and despite the final failure of this initiative to massively incorporate an MNR contingent into the ELN, we can ask ourselves if Che Guevara, for important political reasons, would have been able to share this information he had received from Cuba with the possible author of the essay whose authorship we are investigating here. This, in turn, brings us to the conjecture that the essay's author might be Ciro Bustos, the Argentinian who Che had known since 1961 and who in 1963 and 1964 had participated in the People's Guerrilla Army (EGP) in Salta, Argentina, envisioned and organized by Che himself.[15]

Later, having survived the capture and destruction of the Salta guerrilla movement, Bustos became an important sort of intermediary between Che and various Argentinian left-wing groups who supported the experience of the EGP and who in 1967 continued in the hopes of reactivating a new guerrilla *foco* in the north of Argentina. Supported by this *foco*, these groups hoped to eventually build an

---

14 On Juan Lechín's project of support for Che's guerrilla movement, cf. the messages sent to Che from Cuba in the section "Mensajes Enviados o por Enviar" in Ernesto Guevara, *El Che en Bolivia: Documentos y Testimonios*, Vol. II, La Razón, La Paz, 2005, pp. 256–258, as well as the interview "Juan Lechín Oquendo: Los objetivos siguen vigentes," in *El Che en Bolivia: Documentos y Testimonios*, Vol. V, La Razón, La Paz, 2005, pp. 152–154.

15 On the Salta guerrilla war of the EGP, a project directly conceived of, organized, and promoted by Che Guevara and intended to be implemented in an *initial* phase by his friend and close collaborator, the Argentinian journalist Jorge Ricardo Masetti, and later to be personally led by Che himself, cf. Gabriel Rot, *Los orígenes perdidos de la guerrilla en la Argentina*, Waldhuter Editores, Buenos Aires, 2010. Unfortunately, this guerrilla movement would eventually be discovered, repressed, and destroyed in that initial phase, preventing Che from joining it.

Argentinian-Bolivian guerrilla corridor that would connect the activities of two or more *focos* located in the northern Argentinian provinces of Salta and Jujuy and their neighboring areas of the Bolivian southwest; precisely where the ELN, led by Che, would install itself. It was in this role of intermediary between Guevara and the Argentinian left groups, and in connection to the project of relaunching an Argentinian guerrilla movement to fight in parallel to the ELN in Bolivia, that Ciro Bustos would visit the ELN's encampments in March and April of 1967, immediately prior to his detention in Muyupampa by the Bolivian military.

The problem with this conjecture is that while Che did indeed have great confidence in Ciro Bustos—which could have made it possible for him to entrust Bustos with this secret, sensitive information on Lechín and the MNR regarding the building of a new Argentinian *foco* and an Argentina-Bolivia guerrilla corridor—the dates of Bustos's visits with the ELN and his arrest by the Bolivian Army fall *prior* to Che receiving that information. Bustos leaves the guerrilla campaign in April 1967 and is captured on April 20, while Che only receives news of Lechín and the possible contingent of MNR cadres in May. It is therefore difficult to imagine that Ciro Bustos could be the author we are looking for. Furthermore, and sadly, the great trust which Che placed in Bustos would later be revealed to be misplaced: following his capture, Bustos would betray the ELN by making drawings of each of its members for the Bolivian Army, thus enabling the Army to identify and persecute them. In light of these facts, Bustos's nickname in the Salta guerrilla campaign—*pan blanco*, "white bread," for his dithering and general lack of firmness—rings true.[16]

Beyond, then, the impossibility of the author's essay being Tamara Bunke or Ciro Bustos, we believe that it remains true that this author

---

16 On Ciro Bustos's personality, his role in the guerrilla campaign of the EGP, and his abovementioned nickname and the reasons that explain it, cf. Héctor Jouvé, "Entrevista a Héctor Jouvé," in the journal *Lucha armada en la Argentina*, Vol. 1, No. 2, 2005, pp. 46–61. See also Bustos's own (in our view failed and unsustainable) attempts at justifying his betrayal of the ELN in Ciro Bustos, *Che Wants to See You: The Untold Story of Che Guevara*, Verso, London, 2013; and Jaime Padilla, "Ciro Bustos: el sueño revolucionario del Che era Argentina," in the Archivo Chile of the Centro de Estudios Miguel Enríquez, at https://www.archivochile.com.

must have been extremely well informed, both on the ELN's internal composition and the personal political histories of each of its members, as well as on the organization's links with Cuba and the projects of intermediation and feedback between Cuba and the ELN. In other words, the logical conclusion of these first comparisons between the text and its context is that the author must have themselves *belonged* to the ELN or at least have been so closely tied to the ELN as to have access to and knowledge of secret, encoded, and closely guarded communications between the ELN and the rebel island.

A second interesting lead or clue is the fact that the article in question cites Regis Debray's *Revolution in the Revolution?*, published in Havana in January of 1967; published, in other words, only a few short months before being referenced in the essay. We must remember that in those days neither the internet nor social media yet existed, making the process of disseminating books published in any part of the world much more difficult. If, therefore, we have proposed that the author we are searching for was (very likely) themselves a member of the ELN, we can then ask ourselves: who within the ELN who had begun to work and implant themselves in the Bolivian jungle since November 1966 could have possessed a copy of Debray's book, and furthermore could have already read that book in order to cite it in "Bolivia: Analysis of a Situation"?

The answer points us to the visit of Regis Debray to the guerrilla camp, where he met with Che Guevara on March 20, 1967, personally giving Che a copy of *Revolution in the Revolution?* This copy, annotated with Che's critical notes, comments, and underlines, has survived to the present and is currently stored in the archives of the Bolivian Army.[17]

17 On Regis Debray's arrival in the guerrilla camp, cf. *El Che en Bolivia: Documentos y Testimonios*, Vol. I, op. cit., pp. 84–85 and 98. The book *¿Revolución en la Revolución?* is included in Regis Debray, *Ensayos sobre América Latina*, Ediciones Era, Mexico, 1971, pp. 163–260. This same book also includes Debray's "Carta a sus amigos," in which Debray mentions that Che did *not* agree with several of the theses laid out in *Revolution in the Revolution?*, considering, for example, its criticisms of the Communist Parties of Latin America to be very faint-hearted. Furthermore, Che would surely not have shared Debray's delirious thesis that military aspects would have to take precedence over political aspects in the new revolutionary movements; or that the mountains "proletarianize" even bourgeois individuals and that the city makes even proletarians "bourgeois," among other highly debatable theses presented in the book.

Che reads *Revolution in the Revolution?* through the end of March and the beginning of April. In addition to annotating the book and adding his critical commentary, he decides to pass it around among the guerrillas of the ELN and to organize a short course to collectively critique and discuss it, which begins on April 12, 1967. This second lead—the Regis Debray quote—thus represents a piece of support for the conjecture that the essay's author was a member of the ELN and was familiar with Debray's book (published only a few months earlier in Cuba, in the Casa de Las Américas's *Cuadernos* series) thanks to its collective circulation and discussion in the course which Che himself taught.

It is very likely that in this course Che would have pointed out and criticized the multiple exaggerations and distortions which Debray makes of the theses set out by Che in his celebrated *La Guerra de Guerrillas* (published in English as *Guerrilla Warfare*). Over time, these distortions and exaggerations would sadly but logically become the renegade, traitorous postures that Debray openly held in later years.

Who, then, could this reader of Debray's book—who would have first seen and discussed the book in the ELN, later citing it in their essay on the Bolivian situation—have been? We believe that *Revolution in the Revolution?* would have been much more interesting to the *Cuban* members of the ELN than its Bolivian militants. This is not only because the book had just been published in Cuba, but also and mainly because it essentially seeks to be a political and theoretical justification for the "theory of the guerrilla *foco*," which Debray claimed would be the Cuban Revolution's great theoretical and epistemological contribution to the new revolutionary movements of Latin America.

The Cubans' greater interest in this book allows us to conjecture that the author we are searching for may be Harry Villegas (alias Pombo), the Cuban who accompanied Che both in his struggle in the Congo as well as the guerrilla campaign in Bolivia. Villegas miraculously

---

On the copy of this book, annotated in Che's own hand, which has survived until the present in the archives of the Bolivian Army, cf. *El Che en Bolivia: Documentos y Testimonios*, Vol. II, op. cit., p. 267.

escaped the final military encirclement in October 1967, becoming one of the few survivors of the Ñancahuazú guerrilla campaign.

And as Harry Villegas was the author of another diary of the activities of the guerrilla movement led by Che, as well as one of Che's closest and most constant Cuban comrades, he might also be the real figure concealed behind the pseudonym of Ojarikuj Runa. Although if this were the case, it would be unclear why Villegas would not have revealed his authorship of "Bolivia: Analysis of a Situation" after the experience of the ELN (which he survived) had definitively come to an end (Villegas considered joining the successor movement to the ELN and worked with Inti Peredo to organize it; this project was eventually frustrated by Peredo's assassination in La Paz in 1969).

Furthermore, similarly to the case of Tamara Bunke and the traitor Ciro Bustos, it is important to note that Villegas's general profile was much more that of the practical militant than of the theorist-intellectual. This is supported by the subsequent political and personal path that Villegas would follow after 1967, becoming an important military cadre of the Cuban Revolution and participating in various internationalist missions to Angola. He was finally named Brigadier General of the Revolutionary Armed Forces of Cuba and Political Section Chief of the Western Army, in addition to being recognized as a Hero of the Republic of Cuba. His was a profile of more practical militancy which seems to disprove the conjecture of his authorship of the essay we examine here.[18]

Additionally, we must note that it is clear that the author of "Bolivia: Analysis of a Situation" was quite well acquainted with the contemporary history of Bolivia, as well as its social situation in general. In contrast, Villegas himself recognizes that "it is not easy for one to assimilate a culture" different to one's own, because for this "one needs to have a base. That requires people with broad knowledge, capable of assimilating it," and it was for this reason that in Bolivia, Che

18 On Harry Villegas, who was Che's bodyguard for many years and accompanied Che not only on all of his military campaigns—from the Sierra Maestra and Las Villas in Cuba to the Congo and finally to Bolivia—but also in Che's work as Cuba's Minister of Industry, cf. Harry Villegas, *Pombo: Un hombre de la guerrilla del Che: Diario y Testimonios Inéditos*, Ediciones Colihue, Buenos Aires, 2007.

"struggled with us so that we would interpret the Indian, the way the Indian understood the world, his way of life, his rich history. We didn't have that, despite experiencing a revolutionary process. Che studied the Bolivian's tradition of militancy [...] he went looking for it, and it was one of the things he explained to us. Che knew the Indian's characteristics, like he knew those of the Cuban peasant." This confirms, then, that we must discard the conjecture of Harry Villegas as the possible author who signed with the pseudonym of Ojarikuj Runa.[19]

A Pseudonym in Search of Its Creator

There is a third print or trace we can identify in "Bolivia: Analysis of a Situation" which also seems to confirm the hypothesis that the article's author was a member of the ELN. This is the precise and detailed description of what the essay calls "the theater of operations," a description on pages 217 and 218 of the article which situates the geographical coordinates. Departments, towns, cities, and even railroad lines and oil hubs in the specific setting of the ELN's presence and military activities. This is, in other words, a whole series of truly strategic and foundational information which it seems unlikely that any analyst *external* to the guerrilla organization in July 1967 could have known in such detail. The same holds true even if that analyst were a Bolivian who was previously familiar with the area or who had access to such specific, privileged information, which perhaps could have only come from truly well-informed journalists or individuals linked to General Barrientos's own army.

Why? Because in June of 1967, the epicenter of guerrilla activity in Ñancahuazú—where the first guerilla encampment had been established and where the farm had been bought that served as the material base for launching the entire initiative—was a location known only to the ELN's own members. The article emphasizes this epicenter's closeness to the oil hub of Camiri, at the time the *main* oil hub of the entire

19 The original Spanish versions of the quotes included in this paragraph are found in Harry Villegas, *Junto a Che Guevara: Entrevistas a Harry Villegas (Pombo)*, Pathfinder Press, New York, 2010, pp. 13 and 14.

country, implicitly positing this city as a possible strategic conquest. Were it to come under the control of the guerrillas, Camiri could give the ELN an enormous military, political, and maneuverability advantage: this emphasis only makes sense in the logic of the ELN's combatants, not that of a social analyst in general. The same is true of the information on the existence within the guerrilla zone of operations of two rail lines that enabled easy connection to Argentina and Brazil, as well as to La Paz on the Bolivian side of the border. It is difficult to imagine that an outsider to the Bolivian guerrilla would find this information at all relevant.

Likewise, it is difficult to imagine that someone outside the ELN would highlight the contiguity of this theater of operations with the Andes mountains, which a few years earlier the Cubans had described as the future Sierra Maestra of all of South America. All of these different points of emphasis only take on meaning for someone *inside* the ELN and who, for example, would want to communicate to all Bolivians and Latin Americans where the *general* geographic space of the ELN's activity and struggles was: in this way, Bolivians who sympathized with the ELN's cause could join its ranks directly. At the same time, communicating this location would open the door so that support, contacts, and practical solidarity from militants or movements from other countries in Latin America would be able to establish the bridges and practical links necessary for sustaining and supporting that armed and radical Bolivian guerrilla movement.

It is also important to emphasize the fact that after underlining the strategic advantages of the specific geographic location of the ELN's theater of operations, the article evokes the idea that it seemed as if "all of Bolivia's revolutionaries [...] sought Bolivia's truth elsewhere. However, new winds are blowing over the soil of the Americas and a symbol reaches every corner" (p. 216). Doubtless, this alludes to the general impact of the Cuban Revolution across Latin America; later, the author quotes a speech which asks: "Who are the men who will lead the revolution on this Continent?" (pp. 216–217). In this way, it is clear that the author of the essay we are glossing is attempting to make clear the *continental and Latin American* scope and objective of the struggle undertaken by the ELN. While it is true that one of the central objectives of this

Bolivian guerrilla movement is to promote and strengthen the revolution in Bolivia itself, as well as to take power in Bolivia, it is just as evident that while this objective is important, it is not the only or even the *primary* objective of the guerrilla campaign which has already begun.

In order to better understand this point, and as we have already noted, we should recall again that Che Guevara was always very clear and explicit in regard to his primary objective in promoting and leading the guerrilla struggle in Bolivia: the creation of a second and even third new Vietnam on Latin American soil. These new Vietnams would encompass *all* of Latin America and would be capable of organizing and unleashing a true *continental* Latin American struggle against Yankee imperialism. In light of this point, it becomes important that the essay notes that the chosen theater of operations is well-connected by railroad to both Argentina and Brazil. Once the installation of the guerrilla movement in the Bolivian southwest was affirmed and strengthened, and if, in parallel, the eventual and clearly projected guerrilla movement in the Argentinian provinces of Salta and Jujuy could crystallize and become consolidated, this could make it possible to build a fluid, solidary Bolivia-Argentina corridor between both guerrilla *focos*. This is a project that Che Guevara sets out clearly and that will be the general framework which gives meaning to the different concrete tasks he entrusts directly to Ciro Bustos during Bustos's time among the guerrillas in March and April 1967. It is the same project that will finally be frustrated by Bustos's capture by the Bolivian Amy and his betrayal of the ELN as he yields to the pressure of that army and the CIA.[20]

In being smoothly linked to Brazil, the ELN's strategic geographic location also has a fluid connection of exchange and feedback to an eventual Brazilian guerrilla movement which at the time was attempting to get off the ground in the Caparao region. The Caparao movement's intention was to later spread to other locations in Brazil; sadly,

---

20 On this concrete and ambitious project of building a guerrilla movement in northern Argentina *in parallel* to the ELN's campaign, thus creating the conditions for a possible Bolivia-Argentina guerrilla corridor, cf. *El Diario del Che en Bolivia*, in *El Che en Bolivia: Documentos y Testimonios*, Vol. I, op. cit., pp. 85 and 86, as well as "Mensajes enviados o por enviar," in *El Che en Bolivia: Documentos y Testimonios*, Vol. II, op. cit., p. 24.

it was unable to consolidate itself and was uncovered and destroyed by the Brazilian Army and police in April 1967. It is also important to remember that Che predicted that once the first guerrilla front was consolidated in Ñancahuazú, it would become possible in the not-distant future to open a second Bolivian *foco* or guerrilla front in the Chaparé region. Later would come a third *foco* in the Upper Beni region, which, upon linking with the already existing and active guerrilla campaign in Peru, would enable the construction of a Bolivia-Peru guerrilla corridor. Che discusses this subject and begins to organize some projects around it with Juan Pablo Chang Navarro, alias El Chino or Francisco. This corridor would resemble the planned Bolivia-Argentina corridor and would be a new step in bringing about the transformation (also predicted by Che) of the Andes into a new Sierra Maestra for the entire Southern Cone.[21]

This is a precise, intentional description, loaded with multiple meanings of the guerrilla group's "theater of operations," and is a clear affirmation of the not only Bolivian but continental and Latin American struggle ignited by the ELN. In our opinion, it is a description that can only have been made by one of the ELN's own members or by someone closely linked to its concrete, everyday activities. In other words, its author would have been a person belonging to the ELN's urban support network or to the circle of immediate and direct contacts established

---

21 On the Caparao guerrilla campaign and its relation to Cuba and Che Guevara, cf. Denise Rollenberg, *O apoio de Cuba a luta armada no Brasil: O treinamento guerrileiro*, Mauad, Rio de Janeiro, 2001. With regard to the case of the various guerrilla fronts within Bolivia, it is important to note that even in April 1967, Che was very optimistic about the ELN's future, mentioning the high likelihood that a second guerrilla front would be opened in the Chaparé. Furthermore, we know that until the end of 1965, Che considered it to be a viable possibility that he would either directly join the Peruvian guerrilla campaign or establish the first Bolivian guerrilla *foco* in the Upper Beni region, where a farm had already been bought, in order to create the abovementioned Peru-Bolivia guerrilla corridor from this *foco* or front. The heavy blows suffered by the Peruvian guerrillas at the end of 1965 finally made Che opt for the Ñancahuazú region. On the second possible Chaparé front, cf. Ernesto Guevara, *El Che en Bolivia: Documentos y Testimonios*, Vol. II, op. cit., p. 248. On Che's project of joining the already-active Peruvian guerrilla campaign, cf. Jan Lust, "El rol de la guerrilla peruana en el proyecto guerrillero continental del Che," in the online journal *América Latina en Movimiento*, October 7, 2016, at https://www.alainet.org/es/artículo/180807.

by the ELN's primary leader, Che Guevara, in pursuing the objective of consolidating and expanding his audacious project of creating a new and radical Latin American Vietnam. Because beyond the unfortunate and tragic fate of this astute initiative, the fact remains that it was an ambitious, complex, and far-reaching project. Had it been successful, it would have radically altered not only the whole history of Latin America but the course of world history.

This fact is evident, to mention only one element, in Che's breadth of vision and profound wisdom in choosing Bolivia as the initial location of a guerilla movement which would simultaneously be both a Bolivian movement with Bolivian objectives and a truly *continental* movement located in the very heart of South America. Here, guerrillas could build immediate and direct projections toward Chile, Peru, Paraguay, Argentina, and Brazil through future guerrilla corridors. Bolivia also provided the possibility of easily building indirect but important connections to the rest of South America, Central America, and Mexico.

Who could have had this expert clarity and knowledge of the ELN's concrete area of operations, and at the same time of the continental and international scope of its overall project? In our view, there are two figures who might fill these two conditions and who could therefore be the author we are searching for. These are Inti Peredo (an ELN member and one of the organization's foremost Bolivian cadres) and Regis Debray, the previously mentioned journalist with close ties to the Cuban Revolution. At the time, Debray was a close confidant of the leaders of that Revolution, primarily Fidel Castro, and to a lesser extent Che Guevara himself. Let us examine, then, what kind of basis in fact there is for these two possibilities.

Inti Peredo was a Bolivian, born in Cochabamba. From an early age, he joined the ranks of the Communist Party of Bolivia (PCB), always distinguishing himself as a highly committed militant who was dedicated to the cause of the revolution. Working in various areas—which led him, for example, to the Soviet Union and Cuba, and later to direct a Party cadre school in Cochabamba—he eventually achieved membership on the Central Committee of the PCB. He broke with the Party, however, when he confirmed that it was breaking its promises to support the ELN, and when the traitor Mario Monje admonished him to leave the ELN. In his political work, he had worked since 1963 with Cuban initiatives to support both the Guerrilla Army of the People's (EGP) guerrilla campaign in Salta as well as the various guerrilla movements which attempted to set themselves up in Peru, entering that country through its border with Bolivia. In this way, his political work (as well as practical and logistical work) with these projects of Cuban support for Argentinian and Peruvian guerrilla groups (projects directly supported—and in the case of Argentina centrally driven—by Che himself) had clearly drawn Peredo toward Che's positions and particular ideas about the steps that would need to be taken for the general emancipation of all the peoples of Latin America.[22]

Peredo's incorporation into the ELN was therefore almost spontaneous, and for the reasons outlined above Che soon named him Political Commissar over the Bolivian members of the guerrilla group. Peredo rose to the task, and in the personal evaluations he periodically made of each of the ELN's members, Che would describe Peredo as "very good," affirming that he was "an example in all kinds of work" and that he had "entirely satisfactorily" met "the double test of sacrifice and combat," which clearly marked him as "a great combatant." For the same reasons, Che will state that Peredo and his brother Coco (killed in an ambush near La Higuera on September 26, 1967) were "the best Bolivian projects" in the entire Ñancahuazú guerrilla movement. It was Che's plan that in the near future, if the ELN managed to consolidate its first front or guerrilla *foco*, Inti Peredo might be the leader of a second *foco* that would be established in the Chaparé. Later on, Inti might even command the leadership of the ELN when Che left for his native Argentina in order to continue the struggle in his own country.[23]

22 On the biographical information on Inti Peredo mentioned here, cf. the entry for Inti Peredo included in the section "Bolivianos en la guerrilla del Che," and Carlos Soria Galvario T.'s articles "Coco e Inti, hermanados en la vida y en la lucha" and "Inti Peredo: In Memoriam," all available at https://chebolivia.org. See also the literary testament written by Antonio Peredo, Inti and Coco's brother, "Inti y Coco combatientes," included alongside the text of "Mi campaña junto al Che," in Issue 8 of the Biblioteca Laboral, Ministerio de Trabajo, Empleo y Previsión Social, La Paz, 2015, pp. 147–225.

23 Che's evaluations of Inti Peredo and his brother Coco are included in *El Che en Bolivia: Documentos y Testimonios*, Vol. II, op. cit., pp. 221 and 223.

Che's evaluation was so accurate that when the Bolivian Army captures and annihilates the Ñancahuazú guerrillas, it will be Inti Peredo who, having managed to escape from the military encirclement, reorganizes both the urban support network and the ELN itself, establishing the project of "going back to the mountains" and resuming the struggle left unfinished by Che himself.[24]

And although the ELN will suffer a heavy blow with Inti's assassination on September 9, 1969, this will not prevent the launching of the Teoponte guerrilla movement in July 1970, directed by Inti and Coco's younger brother Osvaldo Peredo.

Inti Peredo, then, had direct and first-hand knowledge of the ELN's theater of operations, and also knew the continental and not strictly Bolivian scope of the guerilla movement led by Che. But the problem in pointing to him as the author of the essay in question is that Inti never showed a strong inclination for writing; this is confirmed by the fact that, unlike Pombo or other guerrillas, Inti never kept a field diary of his activities as a guerrilla. In fact, the only book Inti ever wrote, *Mi campaña junto al Che*, is still *unknown* in its original form: it has been asserted that the work that everyone has read and knows under that title is actually the result of a rewriting of the original text and was authored by the Chilean journalist Elmo Catalán.[25] This makes it difficult to accept the conjecture that Peredo could be the real author of "Bolivia: Analysis of a Situation."

The other person who could meet the two descriptions listed earlier (a good knowledge of the area of operations and a clear understanding of the continental scope of the ELN's campaign) is the French journalist Regis Debray. Debray approached the Cuban Revolution when he was only 21, gaining Fidel Castro's confidence and devoting himself to traveling through Latin America to study various guerrilla movements of

---

24 On the initiative of relaunching the ELN's struggle, see Inti Peredo, "¡Volveremos a las montañas! ¡Victoria o muerte!," published in the July 26, 1968 issue of the journal *Bohemia*, pp. 76–79.

25 Cf. Inti Peredo, *Mi campaña con el Che*, Diógenes, Mexico, 1971. The person who has affirmed that this book is *not* by Inti Peredo and that the officially known version which we have just cited is actually by Elmo Catalán is the Bolivian Humberto Vázquez Viaña, who we will discuss in more detail later on.

the semi-continent's different countries. Out of these studies came his book *Revolution in the Revolution?*—in which he distorts, oversimplifies, and banalizes the theses of Che Guevara's *Guerrilla Warfare*—and the two volumes of *A Critique of Arms,* as well as several essays on Latin American subjects included in the aforementioned *Ensayos sobre América Latina.* In his travels through Latin America, Debray visited Bolivia twice before 1967, researching some of the country's important regions. Among many other sources and elements, this research contributed to the reflections and considerations directed at defining where the first guerrilla *foco*, led by Che, could and should be established.[26]

Given Debray's overall trajectory, we can characterize him as a true dilettante; an unserious, chaotic, unprincipled man who went from upholding ultra-leftist positions in his youth to openly right-wing and reactionary stances in his later years, with a brief social-democratic phase when he served as adviser to the lukewarm and limited President Francois Mitterand, taking bizarre ideological turns and swerves over the course of his life. After studying the revolutionary struggles of Latin America, Debray became the author of several bad and forgettable novels while simultaneously studying subjects as varied and unrelated as world religions, the image, Christopher Columbus, secularism, scribes, empires, and purgatory in 89 books with himself as sole author. Debray also sought to establish the new science of "mediology." This chaotic and absurd intellectual voyage—undertaken by a person who has furthermore always been extremely self-aggrandizing, egotistical, and self-centered—prevents Debray from being taken seriously. Likewise, it prevents serious engagement with his particular versions and explanations of his behavior once captured by the Bolivian Army on April 20, 1967.[27]

---

26 The works cited in this paragraph are from Regis Debray, *Ensayos sobre América Latina,* op. cit., which includes his books *Revolución en la Revolución* and *La crítica de las armas,* 2 volumes, Siglo XXI, Mexico, 1975. Debray himself discusses his two journeys to Bolivia prior to his visit to the Ñancahuazú encampment in his "Exposición ante el Consejo de Guerra," likewise included in *Ensayos sobre América Latina,* pp. 275–311.

27 To get an idea of Regis Debray's chaotic and unserious intellectual itinerary, cf. his personal website, https://www.regisdebray.com.

It is then not at all strange that Che himself, who upon evaluating Debray writes that he highly doubts that Debray "will become a good guerrilla," also writes in his own *Diario de Bolivia* (published in English as the *Bolivian Diary*) on June 30, 1967 that it is very likely that Debray "talked more than was necessary" following his arrest and torture. This in part explains the fact that in 1996, Che's daughter Aleida Guevara accused Regis Debray of being partly responsible for her father's capture and murder through the statements and information that Debray gave to his captors and torturers. Another author has categorically described him as "Che Guevara's Judas,"[28] while others have openly called him a traitor and informer against the ELN. While these facts do not directly invalidate the conjecture of his authorship of "Bolivia: Analysis of a Situation," they do allow us to doubt that, in the case that Regis Debray did write the essay, he would have signed it under a pseudonym instead of his own name. We likewise doubt that if for some reason Debray had been obliged to sign under a pseudonym, he would not later have revealed his true authorship and paternity of the essay in order to give himself the leading role and airs of importance which he has always been so fond of, even now.[29]

Moreover, the primary problem that *does* invalidate our conjecture is the problem of the dates. The essay was written between April and June of 1967, and during these months Debray was either desperate to get out of the guerrilla camp, just as Che notes in his *Bolivian Diary*—as the ELN had begun to directly engage the Bolivian Army in combat—or

28 On Che's opinion of Regis Debray, cf. the abovementioned evaluation in *El Che en Bolivia: Documentos y Testimonios*, Vol. II, op. cit, p. 235, and the mention of Debray in Che's journal in *El Che en Bolivia: Documentos y Testimonios*, Vol. I, op. cit, p. 132. On Aleida Guevara's accusation, cf. Juan Jesús Aznárez, "La hija de Che Guevara acusa al francés Regis Debray de la captura de su padre," in *El País*, August 29, 1996; and Germán Uribe, "La traición de Regis Debray al Che Guevara," in the online journal *Rebelión*, February 23, 2008, at https://www.rebelion.org.

29 To mention only one possible example of Debray's permanent zeal for empty protagonism and being in the limelight at any cost, cf. his letter to Subcomandante Insurgente Marcos, dated January 31, 1995, "Mon cher Marcos," at http://www.regisdebray.com. This letter says nothing relevant or significant and was written only to "make himself present" among Marcos's possible interlocutors at a time Marcos was at the center of global attention and, not coincidentally, was being compared to Che Guevara. Naturally, Debray did not achieve any dialogue with Marcos.

was a prisoner of the military. In either case, it is practically impossible that he would have been able to write the article published in the sixth issue of *Pensamiento Crítico*.

A fourth element that can be inferred from carefully reading the essay in question is that its author *would seem* to be a Bolivian national. Reading the text carefully, we see that the author refers to "our economy" (p. 205) and "our national bourgeoisie" (p. 209). Including themselves as part of the Bolivian nation, the author affirms that Bolivians were able "to turn our country from an importer of petroleum into an exporter" (p. 210) and that "as adolescents we witnessed [the] betrayal" of the MNR (p. 211). "Finally, we had shattered the myth!" the author says at another point, referring to the founding of the ELN putting an end to the idea that the armed struggle was *not* possible in Bolivia (p. 216). Based on all of these affirmations and on the fact that the article is a brilliant analysis of the Bolivian situation, it would then seem logical to infer that the text's author is Bolivian. Furthermore, since we have already discarded the possibility of the author being the Argentinians Tamara Bunke and Ciro Bustos, the Cuban Harry Villegas, the Frenchman Regis Debray, or even the Bolivian Inti Peredo, we might indeed imagine the author to be a Bolivian.

However, it is worth remembering that the article appears under a pseudonym because there were important reasons for the author to *conceal* their true identity; this, then, does not preclude the possibility that the author, attempting to confuse the reader and better hide their real identity, was only *pretending* to be Bolivian. But there is another, more audacious hypothesis we can explore: the idea that the essay's author *assumed Bolivian identity* because they considered their true homeland to be Latin America as a whole.

We should emphasize that this hypothesis is no mere speculation pulled out of thin air. The text discusses the appearance of the ELN in Bolivia, and we should remember once more that the ELN was always led by Che Guevara, an Argentinian by birth who received Cuban citizenship and who on one occasion explicitly declared: "I was born in Argentina; I do not deny my homeland [...] I feel, too, just as Cuban as anyone else, and I am capable of feeling within me the hunger and sufferings of any people of Latin America [...]" "I have a greater homeland," Che adds at another point, "much greater, much more worthy [...] because it is all of Latin America [...]"[30]

This point is relevant because one of the central arguments of the traitor Mario Monje, First Secretary of the Central Committee of the Communist Party of Bolivia (PCB)—who, breaking earlier agreements, abandoned the ELN, depriving it of support which could have greatly facilitated its work and even changed its ultimate fate—was that a guerrilla campaign on Bolivian soil could *not* be led by a "foreigner," implying that the entire Bolivian people should turn their backs on the ELN. This was a ridiculous, deceitful argument, to which the Bolivian members of the ELN responded that Che was *not* a "foreigner," but a truly *internationalist* revolutionary, and more specifically a genuinely continental revolutionary.[31]

With this information, another possible inference is that while the author of the article might have been Bolivian, they may also have been a Latin American or an internationalist in the sense asserted by Che, and therefore in assuming all of Latin America as their homeland, they felt that they were on their own soil in any Latin American country. This allows us to venture the hypothesis that this essay's author might be the Bolivian Humberto Vázquez Viaña, brother of Jorge Vázquez Viaña, alias Loro (Parrot), a member of the ELN who was captured by the Bolivian Army on April 29, 1967 and later executed under the infamous "escape law" (analogous to the fleeing felon rule in common law). For his own part, Humberto Vázquez Viaña was a member of the ELN's urban support network, working alongside Tamara Bunke and carrying out various tasks as a link between that urban network and the ELN guerrillas, such as accompanying visitors or members who needed to go to the group's encampments, or bringing members provisions or various materials needed for their activities.

Later, when Che's guerrilla campaign is encircled and destroyed, Humberto Vázquez Viaña will participate in the reorganization and

---

30 Che made these statements at the Punta del Este Press Conference on August 9, 1961, the transcribed text of which is included in Ernesto Guevara, *Che en la Revolución Cubana*, Vol. III, Editorial José Martí, Havana, 2014, p. 258.
31 This discussion is skillfully narrated by Inti Peredo in his book *Mi Campaña con el Che*, op. cit., pp. 26–33.

attempted relaunch of the ELN, but only until Inti Peredo is assassinated in La Paz. Later, openly hunted by the Bolivian police, he will take refuge in the Embassy of Mexico. From Mexico he will go into exile in Cuba and then in Paris, later establishing himself in Stockholm and finally returning to Bolivia in his final years, sick and no longer able to see. It is notable that after breaking with the ELN in 1969, Humberto Vásquez Viaña would dedicate the rest of his life to researching the precedents, social and geographical position, and immediate and posthumous concrete histories of the Ñancahuazú campaign. In this research, he attempted somewhat obsessively to find the various "truths" which, according to him, were guarded within the complex project of the ELN in which his brother Jorge died and in which Humberto himself enthusiastically participated during 1966 and 1967.[32]

Sadly, Vásquez Viaña would eventually repudiate his youthful convictions over the course of his obsessive search for what he considered the "truth," stating that his support for the ELN had been a "fixation." In some of his books on the movement, he attempts to "demystify" Che as a figure, although in the end he merely echoes various unfounded and biased criticisms made for many years against the heroic leader of the first ELN. These criticisms include claims that Che's approach to life was "quixotic" and unrealistic, or that he was mistaken in asserting that "the city must always depend on the countryside," or that he was a poor military strategist, or that the area chosen as the site of the first guerrilla campaign was ill-suited for this mission; all of these criticisms have also been endlessly refuted by many serious scholars of Che's life and work. We have refuted one of these ourselves in the previous argument on the strategic reasons for why the Ñancahuazú region was chosen, and these reasons were not at all irrational or wrong.[33]

---

32 Regarding this biographical information on Humberto Vázquez Viaña, cf. Eduardo Machicado Saravia, "Los hermanos Jorge y Humberto Vázquez Viaña," in the journal *Fuentes*, Vol. 7, No. 27, La Paz, August 2013; and Germán A. de la Reza, "Humberto Vázquez Viaña," at http://www.utopiarossa.blogspot.com.

33 Vázquez Viaña makes these criticisms in his extended interview by the journalist Carlos Valverde on the 40th anniversary of Che's murder, and coinciding with the publication of the second edition of his own book *Una guerrilla para el Che*, as part of the series Memoria Activa in two programs likewise titled "Una guerrilla para el Che," which can be consulted at https://www.youtube.com.

However, the hypothesis that the author of the essay we are examining could be Humberto Vázquez Viaña falls apart for three reasons. The first is that "Bolivia: Analysis of a Situation" praises the choice of the Ñancahuazú area as the guerrilla campaign's theater of operations, while Vázquez Viaña himself had strongly criticized this choice on multiple occasions. And although it might be possible to imagine that his point of view on this issue changed over the years, the article's position supplies a first reason to doubt his possible authorship. The second reason is that contact between the ELN and its urban support network was broken in March 1967 when it was decided that Tamara Bunke would remain among the guerrillas as a combatant instead of returning to the city. Given this rupture, Humberto Vásquez Viaña could not have been aware of much of the information contained in this article. Finally, it strikes us as difficult to believe that, given his obsessive search for what he considered the "truth," Vásquez Viaña never revealed his authorship of this essay, if he was indeed its author. Accordingly, we must discard this conjecture.

* * *

Let us go over the leads and clues we have considered until this point. Out of these, and of the failed conjectures we have proposed until now, it is clear that the author of "Bolivia: Analysis of a Situation" was a person who was highly familiar with the histories and political affiliations of every member (or at least the majority of the members) of the ELN. This person was also aware of the project of integrating a sizeable contingent of members of the Revolutionary Party of the Nationalist Left (PRIN)—the most left-wing segment of the MNR—into the guerrilla movement, meaning that the author was themselves either a member of the ELN or so close to this group as to have access to confidential information about its ties to Cuba and its specific projects. Furthermore, the author was someone who had read *Revolution in the Revolution?* and had precise knowledge of the ELN's theater of operations and potential strategic advantages, as well as the campaign's continental scope. Finally, the author was either Bolivian by birth or had chosen to become "Bolivian" of their own volition.

To these various and highly likely features of the identity of the author we are searching for, we can add new small clues, like the fact that the author concealed behind the pseudonym of Ojarikuj Runa freely paraphrases Lenin, quoting his well-known statement that "facts are stubborn things."[34] The author also decisively declares that March 23 is already a "historic day," and from that date on, Ñancahuazú is "a glorious name." Likewise, the author also refers to the fact that a supposed Argentinian "journalist" (very likely Ciro Bustos) described the chosen theater of operations as a "masterfully chosen area." All of these details tell us that the author had a strong personality and an ironic outlook and was strongly self-assured. Who could the still-anonymous author behind the challenging Quechua pseudonym of combatant be? The reader of this book may have already guessed.

Leads and Clues on a Celebrated Anonymous Someone

In order to continue clarifying the identity of the author hidden behind the enigmatic Quechua pseudonym, it may be useful to attempt a second strategy. This strategy is different from the strategy of comparing particular affirmations or elements of the text to information and realities of the contexts in which the text was written. This multifaceted strategy is the attempt to realize an "internal critique of the document": this means a more detailed review of some of the text's main thesis and the arguments that support them, alongside the analysis of particular terms the text uses or of particular ways of interpreting ideas, and even the stylistic techniques used in expressing the ideas developed here. This kind of internal critique, combined with certain tools of discourse

---

34 Lenin's affirmation that "facts are stubborn things," included in his celebrated *Imperialism: The Highest Stage of Capitalism*, was well known and very popular in Mexico, although in a slightly altered form: "facts are pig-headed" (*testarudos*, in Spanish). This gives us a small new lead on the article's author, since "reality is stubborn" may have come from a Spanish translation produced either in Spain or South America, not in Mexico, and that circulated in South America. We can thus infer that the author we are searching for was very likely a South American, as there is no other clue that might lead us to the conjecture that the author could have been Spanish.

analysis, will provide us with new clues and elements we can use to reveal the true author of the article.

Reviewing "Bolivia: Analysis of a Situation" from this perspective, we find an interesting first thesis: it asserts that, more than any other South American country, Bolivia presents the most mature *objective conditions* for the creation of a profound social revolution. This revolution, furthermore, will come from the acceptance and immediate practical implementation of armed struggle (pgs. 205 & 219). In this regard, it is well known that this subject—the subject of what the necessary and most favorable conditions for radical social revolution *are*—dates directly back to Lenin, who responded to this basic question (which all true revolutionaries must ask themselves) in his own theory of revolution on the basis of the Russian Revolution. However, this particular formulation of the issue—the specific question of what the necessary *objective* and *subjective* conditions are for carrying out a successful revolution—is actually typical of the debates and analysis of the revolutionaries and militants of the 1960s. The question, then, is: who popularized, across Latin America, the concept of objective and subjective conditions for the revolution? In our view, the person who did this is the same person who authored "Bolivia: Analysis of a Situation."

Another interesting thesis, relatively uncommon among contemporary analysts who addressed Bolivia, insists not only that Bolivia is an economically dependent country, but also that its economic dependency largely results from the fact that it is a *single-product* economy: an almost-exclusive producer of tin. This condition makes Bolivia tied and highly subordinated to the few buyers on the world market who for the most part monopolize the purchase, processing, and transformation of raw tin into finished products.

While it is true that the issue of the structural economic dependency of all of Latin America was a common topic for researchers in Latin American issues (so much so that it gave rise in the 1970s to the brilliant intellectual current of Latin American dependency theory),[35]

---

35 We would go so far as to say that, in terms of a current or intellectual tendency, dependency theory is perhaps the *most important* theoretical contribution that Latin America made to the voyage of the social sciences in the entire twentieth century. It is therefore not a coincidence that this theory was a major influence on the work

it was not at all common to casually and so directly link this structural dependency to the fact that the countries of Latin America were
single-product economies. This provocative and original hypothesis
leads us to ask: who laid out this idea of linking monoproduction to
Latin America's deep economic dependence? The answer, again, is that
the person who did this was the person who likely took Ojarikuj Runa
as their pseudonym.

The third idea that should be noted from the text is its sharply *critical* and radically *anti-capitalist* posture toward the Bolivian Revolution
of 1952 in general, and in particular toward the agrarian reform carried out by that revolution. While a great part of the Latin American
left showered praise upon the Revolution of 1952 and its consequent
agrarian reform, "Bolivia: Analysis of a Situation" characterizes that
revolution as bourgeois, timid, and limited. While the revolution began
as socially progressive, the essay says, it quickly reneged on its origins,
walking back its radical positions and submitting again to US imperialism while turning its back on the people, deceiving and exhaust-
ing them until provoking the military coup d'état of 1964. In line with
this general characterization, the essay also criticizes the lukewarm
agrarian reform of the Bolivian Revolution, affirming that while it
did eliminate some of the feudal characteristics which persisted in
the Bolivian countryside, it left the great capitalist latifundios (large
estates) standing as it created and propagated minifundios, which it
left without technical assistance, stimulus policies, or any of the social
or economic conditions favorable to the consolidation and growth of
these smallholdings. All of this, according to the essay, was a result of
the fact that that timid and incomplete reform was *not* carried out by a
socialist revolution that would have designed it as a likewise socialist
agrarian reform. This itself raises a question: in the 1970s, which author
maintained that radical anti-capitalist posture in characterizing the
Revolution of 1952 and its corresponding agrarian reform? Everything

of Immanuel Wallerstein and that it continues to be taught in European and US
universities as Latin America's greatest contribution to modern-day social sciences.
On dependency theory, cf. (to cite only two of its most notable authors) André
Gunderfrank, *América Latina: Subdesarrollo y Revolución*, Ediciones Era, Mexico, 1980;
and Ruy Mauro Marini, *Dialéctica de la Dependencia*, Ediciones Era, Mexico, 1974.

leads us to conjecture that it was the same author who took the nom de plume of Ojarikuj Runa.

Another important idea that underlies several of the article's central arguments, and which is furthermore directly linked to the previous idea, is that of the centrality of the *peasantry* within the various struggles surrounding the conquest of state power in Bolivia. The peasantry's leading role in determining the fate of the Bolivian nation is apparent both in inter-bourgeois struggles for control of the state apparatus and in defining the possible project of the radical revolution directly promoted by the ELN. The peasantry's new role and importance as the *decisive* actor in achieving a true radical transformation of Bolivia is also one of the topics broadly disseminated by the Marxists and revolutionaries of the 1970s.

It should be noted that one of the most important problems posed by Marxists after World War II had to do with *who* would be the main revolutionary subjects in the countries of what was then called the Third World. In these countries, the working class was always sparse and represented a small minority of the population, whereas the largest exploited class was overwhelmingly the peasantry. This was a vital question for the revolutionary Marxists of the time; some decades earlier, Lenin had solved the same problem by proposing and creating an alliance between the Bolshevik Party and the Left Socialist-Revolutionaries (also called the SRs). Lenin's solution, in other words, was to form a worker-peasant alliance under the hegemony of the Russian Social Democratic Labor Party.

For his part, Mao Zedong would assert that the *industrial* proletariat was the leading group of the revolution. However, Mao emphasized that within the peasantry there was a *rural* proletariat which, alongside the poor peasants who formed part of the Chinese semi-proletariat, represented the most exploited group of peasants; together, the rural proletariat and poor peasants made up the *majority* group in the countryside. This fact would lead them to clearly support the revolution led by the industrial proletariat. For their own part, the author of the article we deal with here seems to assume that the leading role in the revolution in Bolivia (a predominantly agricultural country, like all of Latin America) would be played at first and even generally by the peasantry.

This would justify the establishment of the ELN as a rural, not urban, guerrilla movement, as well as the idea that the always-strategic Bolivian mining proletariat would later completely and organically support that revolutionary peasants' movement which the ELN was beginning to develop.[36]

This then leads us to ask: in the Latin America of the 1970s, what author developed and broadly disseminated this thesis of the inevitable centrality of the peasantry as an *initial* revolutionary force and also in general as a *leading* force within the projects of a radical and anti-capitalist revolution of the different countries of Latin America? The most convincing answer we find to this question is that the author is the same person who wrote the article published in Issue 6 of *Pensamiento Crítico* which we have analyzed, annotated, and scrutinized here on the basis of a consciously assumed reading of the *clues* contained within the article.

And that author, in our opinion, is none other than Ernesto Guevara de la Serna, better known across the world by his nickname (or perhaps and in a certain sense, by his pseudonym) of Che. Che Guevara: his world-famous moniker is half pseudonym or nickname, half real family name, and on one occasion he declared that he preferred to be called by that nickname, Che.

If we first summarize the four questions we have made by performing the "internal critique of the document" we studiously examine here, we will recall that it was Che Guevara himself who, in his book *Guerrilla Warfare* (originally serialized in Mexico during 1960 and 1961 in the journal *Humanismo* and later reprinted in Havana in 1961) clearly laid out the topic of the general conditions for the revolution. Che broke these down into *objective* and *subjective* conditions, affirming that at the time in all of Latin America and almost the entire Third World, the objective conditions were *already* present. All that was necessary,

---

36 On Vladimir Ilyich Lenin's position in regard to this problem, cf. for example, V. I. Lenin, "Primer Congreso de Diputados Campesinos de toda Rusia (mayo de 1917)," in *Obras Escogidas en tres tomos*, Vol. II, Editorial Progreso, Moscow, n.d., pp. 143–164. Mao Zedong's position can be consulted in Mao Zedong, "Análisis de las clases de la sociedad china," in *Obras Escogidas de Mao Tse-Tung*, Vol. I, Ediciones en Lenguas Extranjeras, Beijing, 1971, pp. 9–18.

he said, was to promote and accelerate the creation or emergence of the subjective conditions. In Che's opinion, this could be done through effective work by a *foco* or guerrilla front that was well planned, organized, and implemented, and this was exactly what he tried to carry out in Bolivia.

For this reason, Che reiterates in another text that "the objective conditions for the struggle are found in the people's hunger, their reaction to that hunger, the terror unleashed to suffocate the people's reaction, and the wave of hatred that this repression creates. In America, subjective conditions were lacking, the most important of which is consciousness of the possibility of victory against the imperialist powers and their internal allies through violent struggle. These conditions were created through armed struggle, which makes more and more clear the need for change (and allows it to be foreseen), and the army's defeat by popular forces as well as its consequent annihilation (*as an indispensable condition of all true revolutions*)."

The same argument is laid out in nearly identical terms in "Bolivia: Analysis of a Situation," using the same logic to justify and explain the meaning of the uprising and the actions developed by the ELN until then.[37]

In the same way, it was also Che Guevara who directly linked Latin America's economic dependence to the fact that its countries were essentially *single-product* economies, producers of a single major export product. This original association was doubtless born out of an analysis of Cuba and its status as a mono-producer of sugar, and Che extended it as valid for all of Latin America, including the region's largest and most developed countries, like Argentina, Mexico, and Brazil. For this reason, Che affirms in one speech that his audience knows "how sugar is in Cuba, how cotton is in Mexico, or oil in Venezuela, or tin in Bolivia, or Chilean copper, or Argentinian cattle and wheat, or Brazilian coffee. We

37 On this point regarding objective and subjective conditions, cf. Ernesto Guevara, "La Guerra de Guerrillas," in *El Che en la Revolución Cubana*, Vol. VII, Editorial José Martí, Havana, 2016, pp. 13–14, as well as "A los compañeros argentinos," in *El Che en la Revolución Cubana*, Vol. IV, Editorial José Martí, Havana, 2014, pp. 182–183. The last quote is found in Ernesto Guevara, "Cuba: ¿Excepción histórica o vanguardia en la lucha anticolonialista?," in *Obras Escogidas 1957–1967*, Vol. II, op. cit., p. 386.

all share a common denominator: we are single-product countries, and we also share the common denominator of being single-market countries." At another moment, he reiterates: "But what is Cuba's fundamental problem if not the same problem of all of Latin America, the same even as enormous Brazil, with its millions of square kilometers, with its country of wonders, which is a whole continent? Monoproduction." This specific and singular thesis, developed and defended by Che, is likewise affirmed in "Bolivia: Analysis of a Situation," which emphatically affirms that "our economy is backwards, dependent, and mono-producing" (p. 205). Once again, the hypothesis or authorial conjecture we are proposing here is validated.[38]

In terms of the radically anti-capitalist critique of the Bolivian Revolution and the likewise profound questioning of the huge limitations of its agrarian reform, which the article makes explicitly, it is enlightening to compare these with Guevara's position expressed even *before* the military coup of 1964, when the Revolution of 1952 was still active and in power. On this subject, Guevara affirms in May 1962 that "in Bolivia a bourgeois revolution was produced years ago that was overly timid, greatly weakened by the concessions its economy was forced to make, totally bound to the imperialist economy and totally single-product, as they are exporters of tin [...] and they have made their Agrarian Reform, a highly obstructed agrarian reform where the clergy has not been stripped of its possessions [...]" These theses and arguments are practically identical to the ones developed in the article referred to here so many times, and as we have mentioned are unusual for the Latin American left of the 1970s, which in general sustained a more admiring and uncritical and not anti-capitalist position toward the Revolution of 1952.[39]

For its part, the novel and polemical thesis that affirms that the peasantry is the primary revolutionary agent of the urgent projects of

---

38 The first quote in this paragraph is taken from Ernesto Guevara, "Despedida a las Brigadas Internacionales de Trabajo Voluntario," September 1960, in *Obras Escogidas. 1957–1967*, Vol. II, op. cit., p. 73; the second is taken from the article "Una Revolución que comienza," in *El Che en la Revolución Cubana*, Vol. VII, op. cit., p. 140.

39 This paragraph's quote is found in Ernesto Guevara, "La influencia de la Revolución Cubana en América Latina," in *Obras Escogidas. 1957–1967*, Vol. II, op. cit., pp. 448–449.

radical social revolution across Latin America and the Third World is a thesis that Che Guevara laid out in detail in *Guerrilla Warfare*. Guevara considered this thesis to be one of his "fundamental contributions" in the field of revolutionary theory and one of the primary lessons of the entire experience of the Cuban Revolution. The idea that the peasantry is the initial driving force of the revolution and later its dominant component is one that Che seeks to demonstrate with the obvious lessons of Mao Zedong's Chinese Revolution, the heroic struggle of the Vietnamese people, the victorious case of the Algerian Revolution, and the struggle then underway in Puerto Rico, as well as, of course, the Cuban Revolution. Thus Che emphatically affirms that "Noting that the [subjective] conditions [for the revolution] are completed through the exercise of armed struggle, we must once again explain that the setting of that struggle must be the countryside, and that from the countryside, a peasant army fighting for the great objectives the peasantry must might for (the first of which is the just distribution of land) will seize the cities. On the ideological basis of the working class, whose great thinkers discovered the social laws that rule us, the working class of America will produce the great liberating army of the future, just as it did in Cuba."[40]

This radical thesis was highly heterodox in regard to all those left activists who in the 1960s continued to defend the idea that the *only* revolutionary subject, or at least the *leading* revolutionary subject, was the industrial working class. The same heterodox thesis clearly underlies the entire argument of "Bolivia: Analysis of a Situation," which specifically justifies the creation of a *rural* guerrilla movement and defends the leading role of the Bolivian peasantry both in the struggle then in progress as well as in the victory of the radical social revolution in general.

Once the considerable similarity is shown between various central ideas in the article and some of the central theses of his body of work regarding these same problems, we can also restate the fact that it is

---

40 The thesis on the Chinese, Vietnamese, etc. revolutions as primarily *peasant* revolutions is found in Ernesto Guevara, "La Guerra de Guerrillas," in *El Che en la Revolución Cubana*, Vol. VII, op. cit., pp. 16–17. The original versión of the quote reproduced here is found in the article "Cuba: ¿Excepción histórica o vanguardia de la lucha anticolonialista?," in *Obras Escogidas: 1957–1967*, Vol. II, op. cit., p. 387.

likewise Ernesto Guevara de la Serna who fully meets all of the conditions we have established in the previous comparison between clues in the text and particular elements of their specific contexts. Because although Che was not Bolivian by birth, he did consider himself to be as Guatemalan as any Guatemalan, or as Cuban as any Cuban, or as Peruvian, Nicaraguan, Venezuelan, or Bolivian as any Bolivian by virtue of the fact that he considered his true homeland to be all of Latin America, and this allowed him to speak about Bolivia and its history as things that truly belonged to him.

Furthermore, no one knew better than Che the *continental* scope of the ELN guerrilla, given this was his own political project and the project of his life. Che also had expert knowledge of the guerrilla group's area of operations, as well as its various strategic, military, economic, political, and general social advantages. Furthermore, he had carefully read and criticized *Revolution in the Revolution?*, using the book to demonstrate to his group's combatants the distortions and errors that could come out of a hurried and biased reading of his own texts, particularly *Guerrilla Warfare*. Guevara was not only a member of the ELN but was its primary leader, which gave him more access than anyone else to the secret and sensitive information surrounding the project. Finally, Che knew better than anyone the histories and affiliations of the great majority of the Ñancahuazú guerrillas, as well as the ultimately failed project of incorporating a sizeable contingent of PRIN members into the ELN. This allows us to supply new elements which confirm the conjecture that the author behind the pseudonym of Ojarikuj Runa is Che Guevara himself.

Let us continue. In addition to the arguments presented until now, we believe it may also be useful to compare, from a *stylistic* approach, the final paragraphs of "Bolivia: Analysis of a Situation" and the celebrated final paragraph of Che's likewise renowned and broadly disseminated "Mensaje a los Pueblos del Mundo, a través de la Tricontinental" (better known in English as "Message to the Tricontinental"), whose actual title was "Crear dos, tres... muchos Vietnam: Es la consigna" (The Slogan Is: Create Two, Three... Many Vietnams). We should note that this comparison is based on the fact that "Message to the Tricontinental" could very well be considered to be the general theoretical-political foundation of Che's project of establishing a guerrilla movement in Bolivia as the *initial* platform of a possible *continental* Latin American revolution and therefore as the initial platform of the creation of a second or third Vietnam in the Americas.[41]

The beautiful paragraph that closes "Message to the Tricontinental," which Che very likely finished writing the bulk of in October 1966 before leaving for Bolivia, goes as follows: "All of our action is a war cry against imperialism and a clamor for the unity of peoples against the great enemy of the human species: the United States of America. Anywhere death finds us, it will be welcome as long as our war cry has reached a receptive ear and another hand reaches out to wield our weapons and other men prepare to intone the funeral dirges with the clatter of machine guns and new cries of war and victory."

Comparing this paragraph, which is marked by exceptional beauty and literary force, with the four final paragraphs of "Bolivia: Analysis of a Situation," written perhaps in June or April of 1967, various terms catch the eye for being *identical*, used sometimes in a slightly different sense and other times in almost identical senses to those presented in the text of the message to the Tricontinental. One of these is the idea of action as a "war cry," which in the text on Bolivia becomes a "cry drowned by the hired killers," which makes hate grow. This cry is naturally repressed because it is a cry, first of protest and open rebellion, and then a cry of "the militant hate of our people" (p. 220). In this comparison, the clear similarity stands out of expressing the vocation of struggle, protest, and insubordination through the real and metaphorical act of raising one's voice, of letting out a bold cry against the enemy and his injustice and brutal power.

The second term which is used in a highly similar sense is "death." "Message to the Tricontinental" says that death is "welcome," while

---

41 Cf. Ernesto Guevara, "Mensaje a los Pueblos del Mundo, a través de la Tricontinental," in *Obras Escogidas: 1957–1967*, Vol. II, op. cit., pp. 555–569. It is worth emphasizing Che's perceptive view, manifested in his call to "create two, three, many Vietnams," of what Vietnam's struggle against the United States represented in essence and historical-universal terms. This struggle was US imperialism's *first* great historical defeat, and symbolically represented the clear beginning of the current decline of US hegemony over the world. Che's celebrated slogan *anticipates* both of these meanings eight and a half years early.

"Bolivia: Analysis of the Situation" affirms that "we can laugh at death." In both cases, there is the affirmation of a disdain or scorn for death, provided that this death is useful for the continuation of the overall struggle. In the first case, death is useful because it drives new combatants to join the process which aims at achieving radical social change; in the second, its usefulness derives from the fact that out of death and the spilled blood it implies "will be born our country, a different country" where the Indians of Bolivia will finally be free. This attitude of devaluing death's importance, and of joking and mockery in the face of death, reminds us of the profound wisdom of the neo-Zapatistas who describe themselves as those "who had to die in order to live"; in other words, those who had to kill their old lives of submission, obedience, and resignation and risk their own real lives to be able to live lives of dignity, of struggle, of resistance and rebellion. Because only those who are not afraid to die can defend and affirm life without obstacles and without concessions or limitations.[42]

Four specific terms are used in "Message to the Tricontinental." These are: "hand"; the verb "to wield" (*empuñar*, in Spanish); and "weapons"; which further on become the clatter of "machine guns." These four terms reappear in the 1967 article on Bolivia as a "rifle in one's hand" and later the "rifle wielded by a guerrilla." Later, instead of speaking generically of weapons, the text refers several times to "rifles" and once to "machine guns," speaking in the latter case of "the rifles and machine guns of the workers." Once again, it seems that while many authors of the 1970s discussed armed struggle in general and sometimes used rifles as a metaphor—in the sense of the well-known Maoist maxim that "power grows out of the barrel of a rifle"—very few metaphorized or alluded to that armed struggle in the language of *machine guns* and their clatter. Indeed, Che may have been the only author to have done so. And it may have been Che himself who popularized the expression

---

42 On this wise and dignified neo-Zapatista movement and these profound approaches, allow me to direct the reader to my own texts: Carlos Antonio Aguirre Rojas, *Mandar Obedeciendo: Las lecciones políticas del neozapatismo mexicano*, Contrahistorias, 14th edition, Mexico, 2018; *La Tierna Furia: Nuevos ensayos sobre el neozapatismo mexicano*, Contrahistorias, 5th edition, Mexico, 2019; and *Theory of Power. Marx, Foucault, Neozapatismo*, Peter Lang, New York, 2021.

of "wielding" rifles and arms or fighting with these "in one's hand," as
these expressions were not common in Latin America before the publication of his texts.

To conclude this stylistic comparison, we can also mention two
metaphors which the article on Bolivia uses and which we also find
in certain texts by Che. The first metaphor is the fundamental role of
"consciousness" in the struggle and its quality as an instrument or
weapon greater than almost any other. In this way, in the face of imperialism and its Bolivian allies, who possess technique, helicopters, and
napalm, the article proudly deploys its challenge: the masses and their
movements and guerrillas (in other words, you and I), "have consciousness, and this rifle cuts down a gringo or a criollo traitor just the same"
(p. 220). Immediately, we are reminded of Che's concise saying: "The
construction of socialism is work and consciousness." He will explain
this phrase amply in his "El Socialismo y el Hombre en Cuba" (circulated in English as "Socialism and Man in Cuba"). In relation to armed
struggle, this saying implies that the morality of a guerrilla movement
will always be superior to the morality of an army that oppresses its
own people anywhere in the world. This is due to the fact that the
morality of a guerrilla movement is based on conviction and awareness, while the morality of an oppressing army is based only on cold
material interest. In addition to that morality, guerrilla movements have
a greater capacity for commitment to struggle, clarity of objectives, and
confidence in their own actions; all of this allows the guerrilla, armed
with the weapon of consciousness, to triumph over the gringo and his
ally, the criollo traitor.[43]

The second metaphor shared by "Bolivia: Analysis of a Situation"
and Che's perspective is found in the phrase that affirms that the Bolivian
people have inherited from their ancestors "a national pride as great as
the mountains of Illimani and Tunari" (p. 220). This curious affirmation, where Illimani is taken as a synonym of exceptional greatness, is

43 The sentence quoted in this paragraph is in Che's speech at the Plenaria Nacional
Azucarera, February 9, 1963, in *El Che en la Revolución Cubana*, Vol. IV, op. cit., pp. 281–
282. On this same point, cf. "Inauguración de la fábrica de galletas Albert Kuntz,"
ibid., p. 8; and "El Socialismo y el Hombre en Cuba," in Ernesto Guevara, *Economía
y Hombre Nuevo*, Ocean Sur, Havana, 2017, pp. 64–92.

repeated in a slightly different formulation in a coded message which Che sends to Fidel Castro on May 18, 1967. This message accompanies a detailed and extensive report on the ELN's situation at the time, which is full of optimism and confidence and includes the phrase "our morale is like Illimani." This curious use of the image of this Bolivian mountain may have been common in the country at the time (or may not have been; it is certainly *not* common today), but it may also have been Che's own literary creation. Whatever the case, the Illimani metaphor remains important; like the previous metaphors, it appears to confirm our conjecture that the author of "Bolivia: Analysis of a Situation" is none other than the renowned Comandante Che Guevara.[44]

The Contingent Motivations of the Celebrated Anonymous Someone

Carefully studying the *Bolivian Diary*, we soon find the following phrase: "the clamor continues, but now on both sides, and after my article is published in Havana there will be no doubt about my presence here." Reading these lines, it seems that our historical conjecture on Che's authorship of "Bolivia: Analysis of a Situation," is completely correct and that we have finally found irrefutable confirmation in a text written by Che himself. Unfortunately, this is *not* actually the case. If it were, our conjecture would *not* be a conjecture; it would be a simple historical verification which furthermore would have been discovered long ago by historians or by Che's various biographers (themselves a mixed bag).[45]

In reality, the article which Che refers to is one we have already mentioned, "Message to the Tricontinental," published as a special Supplement in the journal *Tricontinental* on April 16, 1967. In it, Che states that as he writes, "[...] the armed struggle is going on in

44 This coded message to Fidel and the phrase quoted can be found in "Mensajes enviados o por enviar," Ernesto Guevara, *El Che en Bolivia: Documentos y Testimonios*, Vol. II, op. cit., pp. 248–249.
45 The phrase quoted is taken from "Resumen del Mes" and refers to the April 1967 summary. Cf. Ernesto Guevara, *El Che en Bolivia: Documentos y Testimonios*, Vol. I, op. cit., p. 108.

Guatemala, Colombia, Venezuela, and *Bolivia* [emphasis mine], and the first uprisings are already appearing in Brazil." This statement leads us to conjecture that many, on the basis of this text, will deduce that Che himself was fighting in Bolivia at that moment. Although his personal strategy was that his presence in Bolivia as head of the Army of National Liberation (ELN) *not* be revealed until it was already impossible to conceal, this does not do away with the fact that Che believed it to be important and even strategic to announce in Cuba and across Latin America and the world that the armed struggle *had now begun* in Bolivia and that this struggle was promoted and led by the nascent ELN.[46]

For this reason, Che includes the mention of Bolivia in "Message to the Tricontinental," and for the same reason he writes five ELN communiques addressed to the people of Bolivia. Of these five communiques, only the first would achieve real public circulation, appearing in the Cochabamba newspaper *Prensa Libre* on May 1, 1967. To the same ends, Che writes the "Manifiesto del Ejército de Liberación Nacional al Pueblo Boliviano" (Manifesto of the Army of National Liberation to the Bolivian People), dated April 1967 and published alongside "Bolivia: Analysis of a Situation" in the very same issue of *Pensamiento Crítico*. The manifesto is printed on pages 199 to 203 of the journal, while the article which we have referred to so many times here occupies pages 204 to 220. The contiguity of these texts is by no means coincidental and leads us to wonder if the date of the second text is *exact* or might actually be a date attributed by *Pensamiento Crítico*, which would have postdated it slightly.

---

46 In the *Bolivian Diary*, Che refers to the fact that he had entrusted various tasks to Regis Debray, primarily those of organizing a support network in France to support the ELN: (1) passing on two letters addressed to Jean-Paul Sartre and Bertrand Russell, in which Che asks these men to organize an international collection for the Bolivian liberation movement and (2) speaking to a friend who would organize all the aid channels to provide the guerrillas with money, medicine, electronic equipment, and an electrical engineer. On this subject, cf. Ernesto Guevara, *El Che en Bolivia: Documentos y Testimonios*, Vol. I, op. cit., p. 85. On the broadcasting of the ELN's existence across Latin America and the world, Debray affirms that Che made him "understand that an information mission abroad regarding his presence here and the objectives of the guerrilla movement was as important as fighting," in "Carta a sus jueces," in *Ensayos sobre América Latina*, op. cit., p. 273.

There is no doubt that the ELN Manifesto *was* written in April 1967 after the organization's first battle on March 23 and its first military actions against the army, referred to on page 219. On the other hand, it is noteworthy that, despite being dated June 1967, the article which we presume to have been written by Che makes *no* mention at all of the terrible massacre of miners carried out on Saint John's Eve (June 23), when 87 people were slaughtered by the Bolivian Army. Nor does the article mention the acute crisis of the Barrientos government. In contrast, both of these events are registered and emphasized by Che in his *Bolivian Diary* on June 13 and 25 of 1967,[47] leading us to think that the article would not have been written in June of 1967, but rather in May or even April. And given that it was not published until July of the same year, *Pensamiento Crítico* may well have postdated it slightly.

It seems logical to think that Che may well have sent both texts which appear alongside each other in Issue 6 of *Pensamiento Crítico* to Cuba *at the same time* at the end of April, where they would have been received together by the journal's director. When it came time to publish them, the director would have kept the manifesto's actual date, as it was important and could *not* be changed, while slightly postdating the article—whose content was not as strict in timeframe as the manifesto's—to a few weeks behind its actual date of writing. If the article had actually been written in June, it does not make sense for it not to mention the tragic, historic San Juan Massacre or the acute crisis of Barrientos's military government, as these were extremely important events and were also in large part brought on by the existence and activities of the ELN.

Because if our conjecture that Che Guevara is the author of this article is true—and everything we have seen so far indicates that it is—then this text and the Manifesto could have been sent at the end

---

47 The miners of Bolivia, who held a national meeting of the Union Federation of Bolivian Workers (FSTB) in the small town of Catavi, had already decided to donate a day's worth of their wages to the ELN and displayed clear sympathies toward the guerrillas. This was an important reason for the San Juan Massacre of June 23, 1967. Che discusses this massacre on June 25, two days after it was carried out, and speaks of the acute crisis of the Bolivian government on June 13. See references in Ernesto Guevara, *El Che en Bolivia: Documentos y Testimonios*, Vol. I, op. cit., pp. 126 and 129.

of April or the beginning of May 1967 via the Cuban Renán Montero, alias Iván or Renán, an important member of the ELN's urban support network. Renán would travel from Bolivia to Cuba on these same dates, arriving in Cuba shortly before May 13, the date on which a coded message addressed to Che informs him that "Iván is arriving [to the city] sick." Renán travels to Cuba. Later, Tamara Bunke is forced to join up with the rural guerrillas after her real identity and her links with the ELN are discovered. Given that the ELN's urban support network is largely dismantled as a result of these events and that the links between the guerrilla campaign and the urban support network are broken, it becomes difficult to explain how Che could have sent his article and the Manifesto to Cuba in the second half of May or in early June.[48]

Because while the messages between Che and the Cubans continued through a wireless telegraph after the rupture between the guerrillas and their urban support network, it would have been nearly impossible to send either the text of the Manifesto or the article through this channel. Furthermore, because of technical problems, the ELN was able to continue receiving messages but could no longer send responses. For this reason, we believe that both texts must have been sent with Iván before May 13, 1967. As we have already stated and as can be seen clearly

---

48 Che's guerrilla project in Bolivia had been seriously deliberated and organized with a great deal of time and intelligence for two years before its launch, i.e., throughout all of 1965 and 1966. And although until the beginning of 1966 Che was unsure of whether to go to Peru or Bolivia, in either case the Bolivian network of urban support would have played an *essential* role, as it had already done since 1962 in organizing the failed Argentinian guerrilla campaign initially led by Jorge Ricardo Masetti but organized and planned overall by Che himself. As we have discussed, Che planned to join this Argentinian guerrilla campaign in the future. The urban support network in Bolivia would also have been essential for launching various guerrilla campaigns in Peru, as these often entered Peru through Bolivia, as in the case of various Peruvian guerrilla groups which existed from 1963 to 1965 and which attempted a resurgence in 1967. On this intelligent and well-organized urban support network, cf. Manuel Piñeiro, *Che Guevara y la Revolución Latinoamericana*, op. cit.; Ulises Estrada, *Tania la guerrillera y la epopeya suramericana del Che*, op. cit.; and Loyola Guzmán, "Recuerdos de Loyola," in *El Che en Bolivia: Documentos y Testimonios*, Vol. IV, La Razón, La Paz, 2005, pp. 150–165 ; and "Loyola dice su Verdad," in *El Che en Bolivia: Documentos y Testimonios*, Vol. V, La Razón, La Paz, 2005. On Iván's work in general and in particular on his return to Cuba in May 1967, cf. the entire "Mensajes" section of *El Che en Bolivia: Documentos y Testimonios*, Vol. II, op. cit., pp. 243–259.

in the *Bolivian Diary*, Che assigned great importance to broadcasting the existence and actions of the ELN. This was achieved most safely and nimbly through Cuban means of communication, which broadcast information in Cuba and throughout Latin America. For this reason, Che always attentively followed the transmissions of Radio Habana, and for the same reason he always took great care to keep Cuba and Latin America well informed of the ELN's situation, advances, and projects. For these purposes, *Pensamiento Crítico*—read across the island and respected, followed, and broadly circulated throughout Latin America—was very useful indeed.

Now, it bears asking: why, after Che's murder, did Fernando Martínez Heredia, director of *Pensamiento Crítico*, not publicly reveal that "Bolivia: Analysis of a Situation" had in fact been written by Che, as had the "Manifesto of the Army of National Liberation to the Bolivian People" which accompanies it? Two hypotheses are possible in answer to this question, and both have to do with the sad end to which this brilliant journal came in 1971. The first is that Martínez Heredia himself *never knew* that Che was the article's author. This hypothesis assumes that he received the article and Manifesto from trusted Cuban hands and had decided to publish it simply on the strength of its intellectual quality and its acute relevance to that specific historical juncture. And if Martínez Heredia—who regularly studied Che's thought in his own usual range of topics—ever suspected that Che himself was the author of the article, he may have consciously decided not to reveal his hunch because of the sad end of the journal that he directed from 1967 to 1971; in other words. for the entire existence of that brilliant publication.

The second hypothesis is that, knowing that Che was the author of the article examined here, Martínez Heredia likewise decided *not* to make this knowledge public, given his characteristic personal discretion and his deep conviction in not exploiting Che's tragic death or any similar situation. This was first and in general due to the profound shock that Che's insidious murder caused in Cuba, Latin America, and the entire world, and due later, after 1971, to the sadly abrupt and premature end of the journal he directed.

In order to understand the context of both hypotheses, we must remember than in 1967, Fernando Martínez Heredia was a young man, only 28 years old, and was immersed full-time in his various duties as Professor of the Department of Philosophy at the University of Havana and as a highly active participant at the Edición Revolucionaria publishing house. At the same time, he led, organized, and tirelessly promoted *Pensamiento Crítico*. Martínez Heredia was of a reserved and self-effacing nature which came from his intelligent discretion and firm moral conviction of total commitment and critical but unrestricted support for the Cuban Revolution. It is therefore completely unsurprising that in 1996, he declared: "I know how to keep quiet. I have kept quiet for twenty years, even. That is not a poetic expression; it is a description of reality."[49]

We have already mentioned *Pensamiento Crítico's* great and open sympathy for Che Guevara's thought and action, and the closeness of their positions vis-à-vis armed struggle and respect for the revolutionary movements of the Americas and the world. Accordingly, the shock provoked in Cuba and in the journal by Che's cowardly murder was so great—and the attempts to "appropriate" the figure of Che as a means of self-legitimation were so varied and numerous and came from so many different corners of Cuba and Latin America—that Fernando Martínez Heredia discretely took it upon himself to keep quiet about the secret of Che's authorship of the article in Issue 6. And as Martínez Heredia always knew how to "keep quiet," he never revealed Che's authorship (if he was indeed aware of it) between 1967 and 1971.

Later, in 1971, the long, shining Cuban 1968 came to an end. For 13 years the rebel Cuba's literature, cinema, dance, education, and overall culture had been a shining light for all of Latin America. This gleaming *experimental* period had been experienced not only in the arts and culture but in the society, politics, economy, and even daily and family life of the largest island of the Antilles.

When the Cuban government decides to end this radically revolutionary and anti-capitalist experiment and replace it with the Sovietization of *all* of Cuban society, it marks the end of the rich and multifaceted Cuban 1968. All previous rich experimental research, so

49 Information on Martínez Heredia's work and the quoted declaration may be found in Fernando Martínez Heredia, "A 40 años de *Pensamiento Crítico*," op. cit, p. 240.

innovative and bold, is cancelled in order to install the Soviet model of economic calculation, integration into the Council for Mutual Economic Assistance, and economic dependence on the Soviet Union. For Cuba's universities, 1971 also ushers in the use of Soviet manuals, which Che himself described as "Soviet tomes which carry the disadvantage of not letting you think" and which were merely the expression of a distorted, vulgar, simplified, and caricatured Marxism far from the subtle reflections and analyses of Karl Marx himself.[50]

This end of the brilliant Cuban 1968 and general Sovietization of Cuban culture and society also meant that in 1971, the government suddenly halted the publication of *Pensamiento Crítico*. This initiative was promoted by dogmatic, pro-Soviet Cuban Marxists who at the time had won positions within the Cuban government. 1971 also brought the shuttering and dissolution of the innovative Department of Philosophy at the University of Havana, where Martínez Heredia and several Editorial Committee members worked. After 1971, once again from his posture of calm and collected discretion, it was even less appropriate for Martínez Heredia to reveal that Che Guevara was the author of "Bolivia: Analysis of a Situation." In the 1970s and 1980s, that act could have been construed as an attempt to legitimize the journal *a posteriori*

---

50 It bears remembering that as his own thought matured and he assimilated the experience and gargantuan efforts to contribute to building a *different*, truly *anti-capitalist* form of socialism in Cuba, his initial and generic admiration for the Soviet Union began to change (in the 1950s, this admiration was shared by young people around the world, given the Soviet Union's role in fighting the Nazi hordes during the Second World War). Che took on a much more *critical* and refined view of the Soviet economic and social model, which at the end of his life he believed to be more characteristic of state capitalism than true socialism. On this point, cf. Ernesto Guevara, *Apuntes Críticos a la Economía Política*, Editorial de Ciencias Sociales, Havana, 2012. Astonishingly, this book was published for the first time in 2005, nearly four decades after Che's death. The complete quote on Che's posture toward Soviet manuals, is taken from his letter to Armando Hart on December 4, 1965: "Soviet manuals carry the disadvantage of not letting you think; the Party has already thought for you, and your job is to digest. As a method, there is nothing more anti-Marxist, but they also tend to be very bad." Ernesto Guevara, *La épica del tiempo: Biografía del Che en facsimilares*, Ocean Sur, Havana, 2017, p. 176. On the sad end of the shining and rich Cuban 1968 as a consequence of the Sovietization of Cuban cultural life, cf. Jorge Fornet, *El 71: Anatomía de una crisis*, op. cit.

of its sudden shuttering, which from the point of view of firm revolutionary ethics would have been unacceptable.

It may be for this reason that in 1999, the director of *Pensamiento Crítico* declared in an unusually long interview that "after twenty years of silence [...] there are doubtless many things left to say, but [...] there are subjects and information that have never been published and which it is not up to me to divulge, it seems, as long as this long struggle that all of us are in continues." Is Martínez Heredia referring, among that never-revealed information, to Che Guevara's authorship of the article on Bolivia in the sixth issue of *Pensamiento Crítico*? Indeed, we think that he is.[51]

Nicknames and Pseudonyms, Collective Authors and Anonymous Authors

"Do you not like to be called Che?" an interviewer asked Che Guevara on November 11, 1963. "That is a false rumor that has gone around," Che responded. "For me, Che represents the most important, most cherished part of my own life. How could I not like it? Everything that came before, my name and family name, are small, personal, insignificant things. On the contrary: I very much like to be called Che."[52]

This interesting response shows us that Che, a man who was deeply consistent in his revolutionary conviction that politically conscious individuals must be willing to sacrifice everything for the cause of revolution (including their personal interests and desires for glory, as well as all forms of individual self-affirmation and self-satisfaction), valued the nickname he had earned through his revolutionary activities and

---

51 This interesting interview was conducted by Yohanka León Del Rio, "Conversación con Fernando Martínez Heredia sobre los 60," in the book coordinated by Rafael Pla and Mely González, *Marxismo y Revolución: Escena del Debate Cubano en los 60*, Editorial de Ciencias Sociales/Centro de Investigación y Desarrollo de la Cultura Cubana Juan Marinello, Havana, 2006, pp. 183–212. The phrase quoted is found on page 208.

52 Che makes this affirmation in "Entrevista con el periodista de la Sección 'Siquitrilla,'" on November 11, 1963, in Ernesto Guevara, *El Che en la Revolución Cubana*, Vol. IV, op. cit., p. 404.

work much more than his institutional and official family name; the name which Che, like all of us, had *not* freely or consciously chosen. And while a nickname is not the same as a pseudonym (as the former is bestowed by others and the latter is chosen by the person who uses it), both are *false stylings* over a person's formal or official, supposedly "true" identity.

This does not impede a nickname (as in the case of Che himself) or in other cases a pseudonym (like Rubén Darío, Lewis Carroll, or Marilyn Monroe) from becoming much more famous and world-renowned than the original and official names of the people referred to by these nicknames or pseudonyms. Furthermore, a person wishing to be called by a particular nickname may oblige other people to refer to them by that nickname, which can thus approximate a pseudonym. In the same way, a nickname may become a pseudonym if the person designated by that nickname uses it as a pseudonym in *a different* social setting or any context different from that in which the nickname was originally created. Likewise, after being "discovered" by others, a pseudonym can become a nickname used to refer to the creator of that pseudonym.

In any case, it is known that Che enjoyed nicknames and pseudonyms: apart from strongly affirming the celebrated nickname by which he is known to history, he went as far as to sign Cuban banknotes with just the word "Che" when he served as Director of the National Bank of Cuba. He had other nicknames and monikers as well: Teté, bestowed by his parents only a few days after his birth; and Chancho (Pig), given to him by his friends and classmates at the School of Medicine of the University of Buenos Aires, which Che himself modified slightly to create his first pseudonym, Chang-Cho, under which he signed the articles he wrote and published in the magazine *Tackle: Revista de Rugby*, which Che himself established in 1951, when he was 23. There was also *mi viejo* ("my old man"), given to him by his mother, Celia de la Serna, who Che was always very close with.[53]

---

53 On the nicknames (or perhaps affectionate and tongue-in-cheek epithets) of Teté and Chancho, cf. Ernesto Guevara Lynch (Che's father), *Mi Hijo el Che*, Planeta, Barcelona, 1981, pp. 22 and 240. On Chang-Cho, the first pseudonym Che ever used, cf. Ernesto Guevara, *La épica del tiempo: Biografía del Che en facsimilares*, op. cit., pp. 30–32. On "mi viejo," cf. the short story written by Che himself in the Congo upon receiving news

We also find the pseudonym of Ramón, derived from the name he used in one of his many false passports and which was the name Fidel Castro regularly addressed him by in letters when Che was in the Congo. Later comes the nickname Tatú (Three, in the Swahili language), which Che used during his revolutionary work in the Congo, and Mongo and Fernando, which various members of the ELN called Che in Bolivia. This last name, Fernando, was jokingly taken up by Che after serving as a dentist for a handful of Bolivian peasants, becoming Fernando Sacamuelas (Fernando Toothpuller). To these various monikers by which Ernesto Guevara de la Serna was called, we can add those that he himself invented and used in his personal correspondence with his wife. Of the names of Che's own invention, we will mention only two. He uses the first in a letter to Aleida March dated November 28, 1965, in which he says he has turned back into the insignificant Sansón Pelao (Bald-head Samson); in other words, he has become the shaven, defeated Samson, stripped of his mythological power. The second, Marshal Thu Che (a pun on the Spanish *tu Che*, "your Che") surely occurred to him during his second trip to China. To this list we can also add Adolfo Mena González, the pseudonym Che uses in the passport he will use to enter Bolivia in November 1966. There is also El Francotirador (the Sniper), a pseudonym under which Che published several articles in the Cuban weekly *Verde Olivo*. These brilliant and endearing monikers or self-given nicknames confirm the little attachment that Che Guevara had to his own official, institutional name.[54]

We must make sure to situate Che's lack of attachment to his own given and family names in the general context of the Latin America of the 1950s and 1960s. The region was comprised in general by governments who, whether in an open manner or a hypocritically disguised

---

of his mother's death, "La Piedra," included in the journal *Paradigma*, Vol. 3, No. 4, Havana, pp. 63–67.

54 Nicknames or soubriquets referred to in this paragraph: for Ramon, cf. Fidel's messages to Che in the section "Mensajes," in Ernesto Guevara, *El Che en Bolivia: Documentos y Testimonios*, Vol. II, op. cit., pp. 252–257. On Tatú, Sansón Pelao, and Marshal Thu Che, cf. Aleida March, *Evocación: Mi vida al lado del Che*, Ocean Sur, Havana, 2018, pp. 136, 141, and 126. On Mongo and Fernando, cf. Harry Villegas, *Pombo, un Hombre de la Guerrilla del Che*, op. cit. On Fernando Sacamuelas, see Ernesto Guevara, *El Che en Bolivia: Documentos y Testimonios*, Vol. I, op. cit., p. 128.

one, always maintained an attitude of repression toward revolutionary groups, movements, and individuals. These governments persecuted, jailed, and sometimes even physically eliminated left activists, communists, Marxists, and revolutionaries in general, forcing the activity of the groups and parties that fought for radical social change to become clandestine, secret, and way of spies and leaks of information to enemies of all sorts.

Thus, in these conditions that hindered their action and all manner of activities, truly radical revolutionaries became accustomed to acting discretely, to not drawing unnecessary attention, and to not revealing their own identities, family ties, or social bonds to those with whom they spent time, but even more so to their comrades in militancy or to the members of the organizations to which they belonged. For this reason, these organizations always had segmented and compartmentalized structures and their militants frequently used nicknames or pseudonyms, in addition to learning techniques for screening, ways of confirming if they were being watched or followed, and methods of distracting police and spies.[55]

It was within this clandestine culture of secrecy and forced concealment of one's identity that Che matured, increasing his earlier detachment from his real name as well as his liking for nicknames, pseudonyms, and monikers. This detachment from his given name also calls into question the spectacular and absolute protagonism—born out of the increasingly acute possessive individualism characteristic of capitalism in its death throes—which underlies the strong intellectual affirmation of the concept of "the author" itself. As Michel Foucault has amply demonstrated, this strong conception of the individual author weakens and dissipates within the so-called natural or exact sciences, giving way to *collective* authorship in the great scientific discoveries of the past century; at the same time, literature and the arts

---

55 This culture of clandestinity and secrecy, and the self-sacrificing commitment of those left-wing militants ("professional revolutionaries," as Lenin called to them in his classic *What Is to Be Done?*) is brilliantly portrayed in Mario Benedetti's novel in verse, *El cumpleaños de Juan Ángel*, Alfaguara, Madrid, 2010.

see a movement from a weaker concept of the individual author to a strong conception of individual artistic authorship.[56]

Meanwhile, the social sciences—with their intermediate and ambiguous status between natural sciences and the arts—constantly vacillate between both tendencies, affirming a strong conception of the author but simultaneously promoting the creation of schools, currents, and tendencies around those strong authors in sociology, history, economics, political science, etc. The result is that in the social sciences, the "I" is more "porous" and "collective" than in the arts but is also stronger and more present than it is in the so-called "hard" sciences.[57]

Furthermore, the idea of the author has always been conceived from the individual, implicitly equating the concept of the author with the concept of the individual author. But what happens if the author of a concept, an idea-guide, or a theory is *not* an individual but instead a collective? It may be that the concepts of the "porous I" (which mingles with a whole current of thought) and the critique of "the hierarchy of the author" (which denies that a given author is necessarily the best *interpreter* of their own work) both point toward the de-dramatization and contextualization of the exaggerated leading role of the individual author in the social sciences. This is supported today when, for example, we see a *collective* author, the Mexican neo-Zapatista movement, create a novel theory of power and a new conception of democracy, as well as an unprecedented form of analyzing the social structure of contemporary societies and a new theory of what current anti-systemic movements are and should be. For this reason, Subcomandante Insurgente Marcos (who has not by coincidence been compared to Che Guevara) can calmly state that he is a mere costume, a fictional character created by neo-Zapatismo to dialogue and interact with Mexican and international civil society during a developmental stage of the movement.[58]

56 On this interesting hypothesis regarding the idea of the author, cf. Michel Foucault, *¿Qué es un autor?*, El Cuenco de Plata, Buenos Aires, 2010.

57 On of the "porous I," which becomes subsumed into a collective, an intellectual current, cfr. Carlo Ginzburg, "Microhistoria: dos o tres cosas que sé de ella," in *El hilo y las huellas: Lo verdadero, lo falso, lo ficticio*, op. cit., pp. 351–394.

58 On neo-Zapatismo as a "collective author," we should remember Subcomandante Insurgente Marcos's affirmation that "Our history [...] is a collective history, a history where there is no room for the 'I' [...] we, Zapatista men, Zapatista women, aren't

Returning, then, to Che Guevara and his taste for nicknames, pseudonyms, and monikers, we can situate this taste in the framework of the general tendencies within twentieth-century social sciences which question the strong conception of the individual author. On one hand, these tendencies undermine the "hierarchy of the author" over their own work, defending the "porous I," the idea of the author who is porous and permeable to multiple ideas which the author themselves appropriates, taking them out of their particular context. On the other hand, these tendencies affirm the possibility (and even the potential greater richness) of *collective* authors over the individual author, as is currently occurring in the natural sciences. But we must not forget that while Che Guevara *was* a brilliant social scientist, he was not merely a social scientist: he was also a committed political militant with a corresponding practical vocation that was as radical as his ideas. This meant that his theoretical analyses always had an explicitly centered clear political intentionality.

Throughout his life, Che Guevara had various nicknames, pseudonyms, and monikers, and was happy to use them. Should we then add the Quechua pseudonym of combatant, the name Ojarikuj Runa, to this list? Based on everything we have laid out here, we think that the answer is a categorical yes.

* * *

But this is only a historical conjecture we are making, though we hope that it is a *justified* conjecture. It is possible that our conjecture will be confirmed in the future, but it may also be refuted. If it is confirmed, we will have grasped a bit more of the thought of Ernesto "Che" Guevara and addressed a text of his that has gone unidentified until now and

---

meant to each be an individual [...] because the word that made us and makes us be what we are and be where we are is the word 'we.' And this is something many people do not understand," in his speech on January 1, 2007, accessible at *Enlace Zapatista* (http://enlacezapatista.ezln.org.mx/). See also Carlos Antonio Aguirre Rojas, "La muerte simbólica del Subcomandante Insurgente Marcos y el nosotros colectivo neozapatista," in *Contrahistorias*, No. 24, 2015, pp. 29–46. On the new theories and concepts created by neo-Zapatismo, cf. Carlos Antonio Aguirre Rojas, *Theory of Power. Marx, Foucault, Neozapatismo*, op. cit.; and "O neozapatismo mexicano e seu impacto dentro das ciencias sociais atuais: seis teses para desenvolver," in *Mouro. Revista marxista*, No. 11, São Paulo, 2017.

has therefore not been included in his regular bibliography. Should our conjecture be refuted, we will be able to ascertain the identity of the author who has remained hidden behind the militant Quechua pseudonym of combatant, Ojarikuj Runa, for more than half a century. In either case, the science of history will have made some progress. For this is how that science works: feeling its way along, through trials and attempts, sometimes taking some steps forward, but other times stepping sideways or backwards. Wherever it goes, it goes always and tirelessly in search of the historical truths which constitute its ultimate objective. The complicated but thrilling discovery of these truths is part of the immense pleasure experienced by all of us who work every day in the workshops of the Muse Clio.

* * *

Appendix
Bolivia: Analysis of One Situation[1]

Ojarikuj Runa

The armed struggle is an irreversible reality in Bolivia: no academicism can now deny its possibilities of development and ultimate triumph. However, to achieve this reality, this categorical affirmation of the correctness of the armed struggle for accomplishing the revolution, it has been necessary to unleash a true ideological battle which will only end with the success of military actions.

On March 23, the date of the first battle, the first action of the Army of National Liberation, men unknown until then not only inflicted upon General Barrientos's army its first military defeat, but through that action buried a theory that had justified, or better said, tried to justify the unjustifiable: the impossibility of the Revolution's development via the path of arms. This theory camouflaged its intentions beneath empty talk where the most eloquent of phrases expressed that "the

---

1   This text is the article on Bolivia commented upon and analyzed in the body of this book's central essay. It was published in pages 204–220 of Issue 6 of the brilliant Cuban journal *Pensamiento Crítico* (published in July 1967). The original version of this publication can be consulted on the website of the Centro de Documentación e Investigación de la Cultura de Izquierdas, at http://cedinci.org.

Bolivian problem is the most complex in the Americas" or that "we are isolated, shut up in our mountains, and this impedes the development of the armed struggle."

Today, reality is stubborn, and no theoreticism can deny the political and military importance of the Army of National Liberation, just as no one can deny the speed at which the contradictions are heightening in the very heart of the military-civilian government[2] that currently holds power in the country.

The outbreak of the armed struggle is the result of a national reality in which all possibilities for the "democratic" development of the struggles of the Bolivian people have been closed. In no country of South America does the panorama offer such a complete maturity as it does in Bolivia. That maturity has given one theorist cause to remark that "the Revolution is bursting from the ground."

The national insurrection of 1952 woke the Bolivian people up forever from their indifference and political lethargy. It was the popular masses who forced the leaders of the "national revolution" to take revolutionary measures: the nationalization of the mines, until then under the power of the great landowners—Patiño, Hochschild, and Aramayo—who were intimately connected to imperialist monopolies (approximately 30 % of those companies' shares were in the hands of North American capitalists). If one understands that, because of its deformation, Bolivia is fundamentally an exporter of minerals and that of these minerals tin represents 70 % of total exports (in foreign currencies), one will understand "the magnitude of this measure."

As for the Bolivian economy, we find profound contradictions at all levels of its development. These contradictions persist as a consequence of our dependence, in a damaging combination, on a symbiosis favorable only to the interests of the bourgeoisie and the monopolies, economic systems which do not combine to form a harmonious whole that makes development favorable. In general, ours is a backwards, dependent, and one-product economy, from the capitalist regime in the

---

2   Barrientos's government is a military-civilian hybrid, supported by the Frente de la Revolución Boliviana with the participation of four parties.

mines down to the forms of natural economy, fundamentally in the countryside.

The nationalization of the mines, a product—or consequence—of the April revolution, was not able to become an instrument that allowed for the need for development to be satisfied or for the exploitation of man by man to be abolished. The most that the nationalization measure did was transfer the ownership and administration of the mines from the hands of the capitalists to the hands of the bourgeois state. In order to satisfy the objectives of development for the common good and do away with exploitation, a socialist revolution would have had to expropriate the mines, and it would have had to possess the corresponding content: a socialist nationalization.

Though nationalization was an expression of national sovereignty, it was not completed with measures that would have allowed for the free commercialization of minerals, primarily of tin. Bolivia's minerals are exported as crushed ore (in bulk). At the time of nationalization, there were only two plants where it could be treated: one in Europe (Williams and Harvey, in England), and the other in Texas City, in the United States (closed in 1956). The Bolivian people became conscious of the need to establish smelting plants in order to control the commercialization of their minerals. Given the urgency of that complementary measure, a genuine crusade was begun in order to pressure the government of the national revolution into implementing it.

The mine workers, in a patriotic attitude unprecedented in the country's history, committed to working for however long was necessary to obtain the resources that would guarantee the acquisition of these plants; their only condition was that they and their families be given food for subsistence. The mining proletariat was ready to make any sacrifice so that the dearest desire of the Bolivian people could become a reality. Following the miners' example, the factory workers ceded a part of their salaries and wages to the same end. The people's awareness was clear: it was the rulers who betrayed the aspirations of national liberation.

One writer[3] has noted the following defects of the nationalization:

3 Canelas, Amado, *Historia de una frustración (Nacionalización de minas)*, La Paz, Bolivia. This essay is much more laudable than the attitude of its author in political practice.

(A) The state took charge of a deteriorated industry whose future was uncertain given the dizzying drop in ore grade.[4] To confront this, considerable investments were needed which private capitalists were not in a position to make.

(B) Under imperialist pressure, primarily North American, generous compensation was stipulated (close to $25,000,000 dollars). Being provided in the circumstances it was, this represented major benefits for former owners.

As smelting furnaces were not set up in the country which would have complemented the nationalization measure toward the objective of economic liberation, which would itself translate into easy commercialization of minerals, effective control of the industry remained in the hands of its former owners. Consequently, there was an increase in the value of the stocks held by the imperialists, primarily the North Americans, who possessed smelting furnaces which were suitable for our minerals.

Bad administration of the nationalized mines through the state enterprise COMIBOL (Bolivian Mining Corporation) compounded the policy of liquidating nationalization as a revolutionary measure. To this, we must add the economic aggression of the United States in placing part of its strategic reserve of minerals on the world market during a rise in prices.[5]

Losses in mining grew year after year[6] to become the primary source of economic malaise. The government proceeded to a policy of gradual de-nationalization, imposing the triangular rehabilitation plan financed by the monopolies of the United States, Federal Germany, and

---

4   Refers to the ratio of pure mineral content to total extracted.

5   In August 1961, production costs in the country's three main mines were: $1.28 (Colquiri); $1.42 (Catavi); and $1.27 (Huanuni). On the international market, a pound of tin was valued at $1.17.

   In August 1962, production costs increased again: $1.6267 (Colquiri); $1.7279 (Catavi); $1.4544 (Huanuni). Valuation on the international market fell to $1.10.

   In 1963, production costs exceeded two dollars per pound and valuation fluctuated between $1.10 and $1.07. In the following years, market prices fell to $0.90 per pound.

6   Total losses in tin sales as a consequence of the drop in prices—itself a result of Yankee economic aggression—from 1952 to 1956 reached $59,873,837 dollars (the national budget hovers between 50 and 80 million dollars).

the IADB. Those who had bragged of being the "economic liberators of the Bolivian people,"[7] those who claimed to have freed the Bolivian people from hunger, doubled back and betrayed the people.

The pressure of 500,000 armed peasants imposed the adoption of the agrarian reform. The peasants seized the land and the MNR government (Revolutionary Nationalist Movement) basically legalized this attitude, decreeing the end of the latifundio system and abolishing the forms of feudal rent then prevalent in Bolivian agriculture. The adoption of this measure, however, did not essentially alter the economy; on the contrary, it deepened its character.

The importance of the agrarian reform lies in the fundamental fact of its liquidation of feudalism and in the incorporation into the commodity economy of a considerable segment of the peasantry who until then had been marginalized not only from economic life but from political and cultural life as well. The internal market expanded without corresponding development. Statistical propaganda was quite different from what reality itself propagated.

It is necessary to understand how the agrarian reform was applied in each geographic region of the country. The western region is country's most demographically dense and its rural areas are inhabited mainly by Quechua and Aymara peasants; here, agricultural labor is carried out via simple cooperation. The characteristic system of land tenure is indigenous community property, inherited from the Inca period; however, great latifundist properties did exist.

In the country's central region (valleys), spread throughout the departments of Cochabamba, Sucre, and Tarija, agriculture reached its highest level of development: here there existed great feudal holdings worked with backwards technology and visited by their owners only on two occasions: (1) the collection of the harvest and (2) sowing time. For the rest of the year, the owners busy themselves with activities which have nothing to do with agriculture.

In the western region of the country, where capitalist agricultural enterprise has a higher chance at developing, the level of agricultural

---

7   Leaders of the MNR.

development is insignificant. It intensified only after 1952, with the establishment of the Guabirá and San Aurelio sugar mills.

The agrarian reform handed over to the peasantry the land which it worked as private property, perilously introducing the minifundio as opposed to the latifundio. With regard to the agrarian reform, in their book *Adónde va la reforma agraria?* Fausto Beltrán and José A. Fernández tell us that "in general terms the agrarian reform in our country has chosen the path of peasant possession of land in order to achieve capitalist evolution in the countryside. However, it has instituted in parallel a system of keeping huge pieces of land in the hands of ex-latifundists and rich farmers so that this land may be worked through wage labor. In this way, the Agrarian Reform Law lays the foundations so that, alongside the small peasant economy, a rural bourgeoisie may be constituted with the necessary means to make itself increasingly powerful."

As we see, there are no defined criteria regarding the future of the agrarian reform and no defined criteria regarding agricultural policy. Land is given to the peasantry, yes, but how is it given? Empty, without cooperation or technical assistance, let alone economic assistance.

The governing party (MNR) believed it more important to leverage the political-psychological impact of applying the measure of the agrarian reform, which allowed it to control the countryside, than to lay out guidelines on the path to be followed in agriculture. In this regard, Fausto Beltrán and José A. Fernández keenly clarify that "the government of the national revolution and its party, the MNR, did not have and do not now have the organic, ideological, or political capacity to steer the agrarian reform and the people's other victories down the right path."

The leading group of the national revolution, represented by the MNR, first gave up, then betrayed its "revolution," to finally end up in a position of shameful submission, continued and outdone only by the current military-civilian government, headed by Barrientos.

The MNR is a heterogeneous party: within it coexist (up to a certain point) both reactionary, pro-imperialist and nationalist, progressive segments; from the most varied shades of the national bourgeoisie to a strong worker, peasant, and petit-bourgeois militancy, who in movement terminology were the "wings." Hegemonic leadership of the

MNR was exercised by the national bourgeoisie at the beginning of the revolution, but this political organization later came to be controlled by the bureaucratic, importer bourgeoisie, which strengthened itself with the chicaneries of "American aid."[8] But the failure of the MNR is not the failure of the Bolivian people: it is the failure of the bourgeoisie; first vacillating, then conciliatory, and finally traitorous.

The policy of petroleum concessions opened the country's doors to the entry of monopoly capital which controls petroleum production on the world scale; the Davenport Code was drawn up by North American lawyers in their New York law firm.

In observance of that Code, Gulf Oil currently holds a "concession" title of 1,414,965 hectares. In December of 1963, total investment in the private petroleum industry reached $113,083,979.

Petroleum concessions were granted against the will of the Bolivian people, who mobilized in one of the most vigorous struggles the masses have ever waged. However, that struggle was born dead, and the Yankee monopolies, who dragged Bolivia into the Chaco War[9] with the Paraguayan people, returned to the country. In this way, the strangling of the state petroleum enterprise YPFB (Bolivian State Petroleum Deposits) was decreed; in only three years, under the direction of Bolivian technicians and workers, YPFB had managed not only to meet internal consumption needs but to turn our country from an importer of petroleum into an exporter.

The so-called national revolution's drift away from its anti-imperialist content—a content imposed by the masses—comes about with the letter sent by President Paz Estenssoro to Dwight D. Eisenhower, president of the United States. The terms of that letter signal the liquidation of the revolution's anti-imperialist character: the revision of petroleum policy in exchange for American "aid." Phillip Bonsal, ambassador of the United States in La Paz,[10] concludes his work as the "tamer of the Bolivian Revolution," subjugating it to Yankee interests; from then on,

8   The author is referring to instances of fraud.—Ed.
9   This war—in which 100,000 men died—was promoted by the interests of Standard Oil in Bolivia and of Royal Dutch (Shell) in Paraguay.—Ed.
10 US Ambassador to Cuba in 1959—Ed.

we had a Made-in-USA revolution. The first worker and peasant revolution of the Americas was betrayed in the most shameful manner.

How far away were the days in which the MNR's leaders, signing the decree-law that nationalized the mines, had sworn loyalty to the revolution and the people, sworn upon their lives. All of that was a return to the past. Many soon discovered the betrayal and began to work again for the revolution, but the rest had already tasted the advantages of power and preferred to continue down the winding path of the MNR. Many were also left deluded by the chimera of deepening the revolution, but the Bolivian people had already chosen their path, which was not exactly the path pointed out by the leaders of the MNR. Strikes begin and a vigorous mass struggle is unleashed: the Bolivian people must be awoken again, and their betrayers must be unmasked.

On the other hand, the right wing of the MNR, captained by Siles Zuazo and Walter Guevara, controls the state apparatus. Paz Estenssoro's project of creating an industrial bourgeoisie is a rotund failure. Loans "of honor" and "American aid" funds granted to government hierarchs in the hope of creating light industry multiply only the number of importers tied closely to Yankee monopolies. The rest prefer to keep their "savings" safe in US and Swiss banks for a rainy day; presently, many of them, yesterday's "revolutionaries" and today's traitors, sweeten their exile with Paz Estenssoro's dreams of industrialization. Under that title they robbed almost $100,000,000 from the people.

The 12 years of the national revolutionary government have been years of frustration for the deceived, swindled, and betrayed Bolivian people. A historic judgment and accounting of that period must be made, and we are confident that it will be made completely only following the victory of the armed struggle.

It is that reality, those facts, that make it possible to comprehend the impossibility of national liberation in the framework proposed by the MNR. Even as adolescents we witnessed that betrayal; we grew and matured understanding that reality; we were witnesses to the degradation and institutionalization of fraud for rank-climbing in the spheres of the twelve-year government. It was an entire era of the inversion of our highest values, in which thieves, demagogues, and thugs climbed quickly toward the highest positions. However, this does not mean—and we do not mean to say or maintain—that there were no honest and honorable revolutionaries in the ranks of the MNR who sincerely believed in the possibility of deepening the revolution; there were, and their only mistake, if we can even qualify it as such, lay in not understanding that that deepening necessarily meant removing the MNR from power. We are not speaking, then, of those who were able to combat and confront Falangist subversion in the first years of the revolution or of those who, with conviction in the movement, confronted the machine guns of Barrientos's air force in defense of the flags of April. We are not speaking of those who died for those ideals, the ideals of the people on the hills of Laikakota in the city of La Paz. Clear proof of this is the participation of MNR militants in the Army of National Liberation.

The military rebellion of November 4, 1964, promoted by the US embassy, was the result of a long period that the army spent preparing to storm the halls of power; to understand its meaning, we must go back to the national and mass insurrection of April 9, 1952. On that occasion, the people in arms defeated the strongest army which the Republic had ever raised. In the city of La Paz, the factory workers confronted the soldiers of the regiments of Abaroa, Sucre, Lanza, Ingavi, Escuela Motorizada de Viacha, the Military Academy, and the Bolívar artillery regiment; 9 regiments in total, with 10,000 perfectly outfitted and trained soldiers.

The national insurrection began on Good Friday; in the first hours of battle, the people stormed the military arsenal and managed to seize its weapons. The cadets of the Military Academy used 105 mm mortars and bombarded working-class areas and the National Stadium, where many revolutionaries who were ready to fight had gathered.

In Villa Victoria, where many El Alto factory workers live, on the Laikakota hills, and among all the mass sectors of the city of La Paz, heavy fighting broke out. On the first day of battle, the army used its military power against the insurgents, but the force of the people prevailed over the weapons wielded by the army of the oligarchs. That army had committed many massacres against the people, and not in vain was it called the "massacring army."

The army suffered a crushing, overwhelming defeat. Nothing was left in the barracks of the oligarchy's army; the repressive apparatus of the feudal, mining bourgeoisie was utterly destroyed.

Following the triumph of the revolution, using weapons seized from the army, popular militias were organized by factory workers, miners, and revolutionary university students. Every workers' union had its own militia.

With the army totally dismantled, former military officers chose the path of exile; those who remained were closely tied to the MNR and the leadership of the local and national police who had fought alongside the people during the April days.

The reaction, defeated in April, raised as its banner the rebuilding of the army. For the first years of the revolution, there was no army. Later, the MNR took on the task of reorganizing the "Army of the national revolution." Only later, when the right wing of the MNR took control of the State apparatus with Hernán Siles Zuazuo, was the reorganization of the state seriously considered. The US military mission understood the importance of this work; silently, without too much fanfare, the barracks began to fill again with officers, and the military academy, spawn of the gorillocracy, reopened. All of the weapons, resources, and technical assistance was supplied by the Pentagon. By the end of Siles Zuazo's government in 1960, there was a perfectly organized army controlled by the Pentagon, with the ability and strength to enter the political arena. General Barrientos, former official pilot of Paz Estenssoro, had experienced a meteoric military career, rising from lieutenant to divisional general in a few short years.

Between 1960 and 1963, Barrientos begins a campaign of penetrating into the countryside with the Civic Action program; using Pentagon resources, he builds schools in rural areas and makes use of demagogic discourse, using his fluency in the Quechua language for psychological impact. Barrientos had already mapped the path that would lead him to the Palace of Government: he had understood that it was not possible to seize power without the backing of the peasants. He completely reorganizes and strengthens the army, with the full knowledge of Paz Estenssoro. At the end of Paz Estenssoro's second government, fulfilling the promise of rotation of power was suggested, a tacit agreement between the MNR's leaders. It was Juan Lechín's turn to occupy the leadership position of the national revolutionary State, but despite this moral agreement, Paz Estenssoro did not plan on giving up the presidency. This was the fundamental reason for the final breakdown of the MNR. Lechín left the MNR, calling a national Convention of the segment of the party which he controlled (the left wing) and founding a new political party, the PRIN (Revolutionary Party of the Nationalist Left), in which he enjoyed strong support from mine workers.

The head of the MNR had been left in control of important and strategic rural groups as a strong base of support for his government. It cannot be said that the army was completely behind him; Barrientos had completed his work and the young officers had gathered around him due to what has been described as a generational matter. On his end, Paz Estenssoro trusted in the old officers who had been loyal until then and who controlled important units of the Armed Forces, including General Ovando. The Bolivian panorama of 1964, however, was different from that of 1960. Those four years had not gone idly by for the army, which was now ready to demand participation in what the officers call "the destinies of the Nation." Perhaps it was Paz's calculations that failed him: it is possible that he may have thought to placate Barrientos with the vice presidency he had been chosen for; perhaps he believed that Barrientos had four years worth of patience while he waited to become president. But the real situation was very different from Paz Estenssoro's calculations. On one hand, he had to confront the rightist opposition, which was gathered around the Falange[11] and had a great deal of strength in the departments of Cochabamba and Santa Cruz. On the other hand, he was facing the working class, which was beginning a vigorous mass struggle for economic and social demands.

May of 1964 marks an important milestone in Paz's fall. Their economic petitions refused, the mine workers declare a strike: incapable of controlling the situation, Estenssoro resorts to violence. The army heads for the mining centers and the miners mobilize to confront them; the two sides clash on the Sora-Sora heights, some five kilometers outside of the city of Oruro.

---

11 Bolivian Socialist Falange (Reactionary party).—Ed.

The results: massacred workers and dozens of soldiers dead, the miners resisting bravely. These repressive actions remind the working class of the "Rosca" and the "massacring army." Paz breaks with his people. In October 1964, the student struggle intensifies in the country following the murder of a student in the city of Cochabamba. More than 20,000 teachers strike for wage increases. The disturbances grow and the situation becomes profoundly complicated. Paz breaks with the Cuban Revolution in hopes of winning the trust of the State Department, jails union leaders, persecutes the left, and "discovers" a communist conspiracy. But all of this was not enough to save him: imperialism had withdrawn its support, and his fate was sealed. Barrientos, his vice president, left the seat of government and traveled to Cochabamba, where he established his headquarters for the definitive seizure of power. Like an attack dog, the army lent itself to these actions, spending weeks, later days, simply waiting for the right moment. November came and greater mutinies were set off. From his headquarters, Barrientos cartoonishly fired off bitter criticisms of Paz. On November 3, the Seventh Division of the Army mutinies in Cochabamba. Barrientos ably puts the finishing touch on the panorama: he resigns from his post as "Vice."

The situation is muddled in the heart of the army. Initially, Ovando seeks to "mediate" the conflict, but Paz finally steps down. On November 5, he leaves La Paz without even notifying many of those who were loyal to him until the end. At the moment that the airplane is about to take off from the El Alto airport, one of his supporters refuses to stay, and practically has to be dragged away so the plane can leave.

Paz was on his way into exile. The same pilot who had brought him from Buenos Aires in 1952 to take power was now throwing him out.[12]

Barrientos entered La Paz "in triumph." The "savior" arrived, wanting to be president; "coincidentally," Ovando also wanted to be president. At that moment, each officer felt like a sort of Bonaparte. The people had also participated in the military revolt: on November 4, they stormed the police barracks, seized weapons, and fought against

---

12 In July of 1946, upon the fall of Villarroel following an insurrection, Paz Estenssoro, then Economy Minister, fled into exile; the pilot of his plane was Barrientos. After the triumph of April, Barrientos flies the plane that brings Paz Estenssoro back from exile.

the military units that had obeyed Paz until the end. This setback had not formed part of Barrientos's plans and forced the Junta to make certain concessions to the people, who had also faced down the General's planes on the hills of Laikakota and El Alto.

The rest of the story is well known. May and September of 1965: bombing of mining centers and massacres in Villa Victoria and Cerdas. Reactionary politics are matched by crime, persecution, and aggression against the workers' finances. Miners' wages and salaries are cut by between 40 % and 50 %.

General Barrientos establishes the Popular Christian Movement [MPC] to support his government. The right goes on the offensive and the traditional parties liquidated in 1952 are reformed. Barrientos founds the Front of the Bolivian Revolution [FRB], in which his party and other politically meaningless groups participate. The Revolutionary Left Party [PIR], self-described as leftist, comprised primarily of university professors, and headed by Ricardo Anaya, currently cooperates with the military-civilian government, as does Walter Guevara Arce, former minister of the Hernán Siles government.

The crisis of the Bolivian economy fundamentally lies in mining, and the military-civilian government has shown itself to be incapable of solving it; it has envisioned no serious perspective of solution. Poverty and hunger grow worse: this is the panorama.

The left parties are reluctant to abandon the traditional schemas of struggle, while the classical conception of insurrection gains ground within the left, and, as Regis Debray says, "it is difficult to repeat 1952 in 1966."[13]

The Communist Party had decisive force in the mining centers and some segments of the cities and countryside. Lechín's party is also a politically significant force. Important symptoms of progress appear in the heart of the destroyed and atomized MNR: faced with the fall of Paz, many honest militants understand the need for action. However, apparently until the end of 1966 there is inactivity, passivity, and conformism; it seems that the struggle of the left parties had been reduced to a war of letters, of definitions; all of Bolivia's revolutionaries, it seems,

---

13 *¿Revolución en la Revolución?* Cuadernos Casa de las Américas, Havana, 1967.

sought Bolivia's truth elsewhere. However, new winds are blowing over the soil of the Americas and a symbol reaches every corner. The need for action is more and more urgent.

Many revolutionary leaders wait for the "political juncture"; many revolutionaries understand that something had to happen in the midst of that apparent calm: "it is difficult to know what the correct moment is to move from legal action to violent action, to insurrection." That question had already been solved by "the strangers."

Actions began on March 23: it is difficult to explain what was felt by those of us who for whatever reason were outside of the country on that day. We only remember feeling something as if our blood had ceased to flow, and we devoured the news cables with our eyes. Finally, we had shattered the myth! The armed struggle had begun, there in our homeland. In that moment we thought of Fidel: "Who are the men who will lead the revolution on this Continent? It may be many cases may be like ours, men whose names have never appeared in print, men who are not even known. But we know too that in the ranks of the people stand those sorts of names who sooner or later, correctly interpreting realities and facts, with revolutionary conviction and confidence in the people, will lead the peoples of the world forth to liberation."

It may be that when Fidel gave that speech in the Plaza of the Revolution, the patriots of Bolivia heard it in the place that the world now knows by the glorious name of Ñancahuazú. Since then, March 23 is not an empty date: it is a historic day. The guerrilla fighters of the Army of National Liberation continue the tradition of struggle of the independence guerrillas who fought for 15 years to win their freedom from the oppressor's yoke. They remember the struggles and glories of the combatants who established the "Republiquetas." They follow in the footsteps of José Miguel Lanza, who founded the impregnable republiqueta of Apoyopaya and Inquisivi in Cochabama; of Ildefonso de las Muñecas in Larecaja (La Paz); of José Vicente Camargo in Cinti (Sucre); of Manuel Asencio Padilla and Juana Azurduy de Padilla on the border with the Chiriguanos (Santa Cruz); of Ignacio Warnes and Juan Antonio Albarez de Arenales in Vallegrande (Santa Cruz); of Ramón Rojas in Tarija, and of many others.

The Theater of Operations

The area of operations of the Army of National Liberation spans areas of the departments of Santa Cruz, Sucre, and Tarija: the first battles were fought in the Ñancahuazú area, within the jurisdiction of the province of Cordillera, Department of Santa Cruz. Close to this area lie the municipalities of Valle Grande, Lagunillas, and Camiri, the country's main petroleum hub.

Two railroad lines pass through this area which link Bolivia to Argentina and Brazil: the Yacuiba-Santa Cruz railroad, which runs through the town of Villazón, reaching Oruro and La Paz; and the Corumba-Santa Cruz railroad, which runs further north and links us to Brazil. The region encompassed by the foothills of the western Cordillera of the Andes and the plains of the southeast is of a subtropical climate, covered in thick vegetation and impenetrable jungle and sliced by rivers full of fish. This geography is rough, with long gorges and canyons. Camiri, the country's petroleum capital, is of the utmost importance to the national economy; from here stretch the pipelines that carry petroleum to the refineries of Mesa Verde (Sucre) and Gualberto Villarroel (Cochabamba). From the latter refinery runs a pipeline to the Chilean port of Arica, where petroleum is exported to the United States.

Commenting on the Army of National Liberation's area of operations, one Argentinian journalist described it as a "masterfully chosen area." The jungle allows for perfect ease of movement among the guerrillas: one can walk without being discovered until one is three meters away. One of the serious problems Barrientos's army has faced is the inadaptability of altiplano recruits to the subtropical region, which creates serious problems that will worsen later on. The army is fighting unprepared in an area it does not know. In order to adapt himself, an altiplano soldier would need profound moral motivations, a profound ideological conviction in the necessity of his struggle: this is impossible to achieve within the army of the puppet Barrientos. In view of this problem, his army has recruited youths from the tropical cities of the country, which has caused serious disruptions in the internal order, bringing unrest to areas far away from the center of guerrilla operations.

The inadaptability of the altiplano soldier to jungle regions manifests first in excessive dehydration; later, he is unexpectedly overcome by a weakness that saps his strength for the normal performance of his bodily functions. Although this illness can be overcome through a prolonged posting, swelling in his feet will lead to more serious problems. Constant biting by mosquitos and the huge variety of arachnids and snakes are demoralizing factors for the altiplano soldier, who is generally not accustomed to tropical climates.

At a certain point in the development of military actions, the army will be forced to move its troops from nearby barracks to the mining hubs and will in this way create the possibility for significant action on the part of the mining proletariat. On the other hand, Barrientos's army will never create a soldier in which it can place full trust. Army troops are recruited via a military service that lasts for two years; most recruits come from rural areas in the altiplano and valleys and are therefore strongly tied to their towns. Currently, the greatest problem facing Barrientos's army is its lack of training and its ignorance of the area of operations, on top of the logistical problems created by the mobilization of 3,000 soldiers toward that region. Military advisory provided by Yankee "experts" and the use of helicopters—also recommended by Yankee officers—is currently that army's main source of hope. However, air support and napalm bombing is completely useless given the denseness of the jungle. The objective of bombing is psychological, meant to pressure the peasants who live inside the area of operations of the Army of National Liberation.

The army's greatest concern currently is set on liquidating the guerrilla's supply sources: General Ovando ordered all sown fields to be destroyed and all ripe corn to be collected and brought to the centers where the barracks of the anti-guerrilla struggle have been established; there are, however, various types of edible plants in that jungle, as well as abundant game.

Given its characteristics and territorial extension, it is difficult for the army to control the zone in which the guerrillas operate, keeping in mind that guerrillas are highly mobile units who can act with great agility. The continuous successes of the military actions of the Army of National Liberation have taken the military by surprise. Its movements are neither disorganized nor scattered: they are movements which appear to follow a perfectly planned military strategy.

In no country are the conditions for the victory of the armed struggle as present as they are in Bolivia, given its experience of mature, consequential struggle. This is a people ready to sacrifice for their liberation.

"Democratic peace" in Bolivia has no prospects. The twelve years of the MNR have been a hard lesson which the people have assimilated and are not inclined to repeat. In these hours, the rifles and machine guns of the mine workers and factories are not yet in combat, but in the outlook of the struggle to come, a whole people are tensed, ready to write the pages of their history that signal their definitive liberation.

There is much suffering in the consciences of Bolivians; 400 years of Spanish oppression that weighed upon our people did not bow us. One hundred and fifty years as a republic have not deformed us. Though it is true that we live up in our mountains, we have forgotten neither the TIWANAKU nor the COLLASUYU. It is true; today green berets lay their boots on our soil, but we have forgotten neither Quechua nor Aymara. We will light enormous fires in the altiplano with altiplano grasses and llama dung and with corn and wheat hay in the valleys, because today the fires are already burning on the plains.

The gray days that break over the mountains of our altiplano are dyed red in the west. In each cry drowned by the hired killers grows hate, the militant hate of our people. Each rifle wielded by a guerrilla holds the dawn that will illuminate our land. Today, they have technique, helicopters, and napalm, but we have consciousness, and this rifle cuts down a gringo or a criollo traitor just the same.

We are a people who inherit from our elders a national pride as great as the mountains of Illimani and Tunari, and we can laugh at death because we know that of that blood will be born our country, a different country where Indians will not kiss the hand of "Hapaj runa," where the Colla and the Camba sing the taquirari or the huayño just the same. But these are dreams for later. Today, the sign that one is Bolivian is the rifle in one's hand.

June 1967

PETER LANG
PROMPT

Peter Lang Prompts offer our authors the opportunity to publish original research in small volumes that are shorter and more affordable than traditional academic monographs. With a faster production time, this concise model gives scholars the chance to publish time-sensitive research, open a forum for debate, and make an impact more quickly. Like all Peter Lang publications, Prompts are thoroughly peer reviewed and can even be included in series.

For further information, please contact:

editorial@peterlang.com

To order, please contact our Customer Service Department:

peterlang@presswarehouse.com (within the U.S.)
orders@peterlang.com (outside the U.S.)

Visit our website: www.peterlang.com

Prompts include:

Claudia Aburto Guzmán, *Poesía reciente de voces en diálogo con la ascendencia hispano-hablante en los Estados Unidos: Antología breve.* ISBN 978-1-4331-5207-8. 2020

William Robert Adamson, *Mine Own Familiar Friend: The Relationship between Gerard Hopkins and Robert Bridges.* ISBN 978-1-80079-485-6. 2021

Tywan Ajani, *Barriers to Rebuilding the African American Community: Understanding the Issues Facing Today's African Americans from a Social Work Perspective.* ISBN 978-1-4331-7681-4. 2020

Macarena Areco, *Bolaño Constelaciones: Literatura, sujetos, territorios.* ISBN 978-1-4331-7575-6. 2020

Franck Besingrand, *César Franck: Entre raison et passion.* ISBN 978-2-87574-601-6. 2022

Robin Burgess (ed.), *FRANCESCO ALGAROTTI: AN ESSAY ON THE OPERA (Saggio sopra l'opera in musica) The editions of 1755 and 1763.* ISBN 978-1-80079-505-1. 2022

Desrine Bogle. *The Transatlantic Culture Trade: Caribbean Creole Proverbs from Africa, Europe, and the Caribbean.* ISBN 978-1-4331-5723-3. 2020

Jean-François Caron. *Irresponsible Citizenship: The Cultural Roots of the Crisis of Authority in Times of Pandemic.* ISBN 978-1-4331-8908-1. 2021

Jean-François Caron, *The Great Lockdown: Western Societies and the Fear of Death.* ISBN 978-1-4331-9535-8. 2022

Marcílio de Freitas and Marilene Corrêa da Silva Freitas, *The Future of Amazonia in Brazil: A Worldwide Tragedy.* ISBN 978-1-4331-7793-4. 2020

Mihai Dragnea. *Christian Identity Formation Across the Elbe in the Tenth and Eleventh Centuries.* Christianity and Conversion in Scandinavia and the Baltic Region, c. 800–1600, vol. 1. ISBN 978-1-4331-8431-4. 2021

Janet Farrell Leontiou, *The Doctor Still Knows Best: How Medical Culture Is Still Marked by Paternalism.* Health Communication, vol. 15. ISBN 978-1-4331-7322-6. 2020

George A. Gonzalez, *Star Trek and Star Wars: The Enlightenment versus the Anti-Enlightenment.* ISBN 978-1-4331-9770-3. 2022

Clare Gorman (ed.), *Miss-representation: Women, Literature, Sex and Culture.* ISBN 978-1-78874-586-4. 2020

Eva Marín Hlynsdóttir. *Gender in Organizations: The Icelandic Female Council Manager.* ISBN 978-1-4331-7729-3. 2020

Micol Kates, *Towards a Vegan-Based Ethic: Dismantling Neo-Colonial Hierarchy Through an Ethic of Lovingkindness.* ISBN 978-1-4331-7797-2. 2020

Sunho Kim, *Inner Mongolia, Outer Mongolia: The History of the Division of the "Descendants of Chinggis Khan" in the 20th Century.* ISBN 978-1-4331-8185-6. 2022

Feridoon Koohi-Kamali (ed.), *Exploring Roots of Inequality in Latin America and Peru.* ISBN 978-1-4331-8989-0. 2021

Alena Kusá, Tomáš Fašiang and Daniela Kollárová, *Retail Marketing Communication and the Consumer Behaviour of Selected Generations.* ISBN 978-1-80079-855-7. 2022

Francisco García Marcos, *Communication in the Analects of Confucius.* ISBN 978-1-4331-9257-9. 2022

Guy Merchant, Cathy Burnett, Jeannie Bulman, and Emma Rogers. *Stacking Stories: Exploring the Hinterland of Education.* ISBN 978-1-80079-686-7. 2022

Marco Micone, *The Enchanted Figtree.* Translated by Beatrice Guenther. ISBN 978-1-80079-813-7. 2022

Matt Qvortrup, *Winners and Losers: Which Countries are Successful and Why?.* ISBN 978-1-80079-405-4. 2021

Peter Raina, *Doris Lessing – A Life Behind the Scenes: The Files of the British Intelligence Service MI5.* ISBN 978-1-80079-183-1. 2021

Peter Raina (trans.), *Heinrich von Kleist Poems.* ISBN 978-1-80079-043-8. 2020

Josiane Ranguin, *Mediating the Windrush Children: Caryl Phillips and Horace Ové.* ISBN 978-1-4331-7424-7. 2020

Dylan Scudder, *Coffee and Conflict in Colombia: Part of the Pentalemma Series on Managing Global Dilemmas.* ISBN 978-1-4331-7568-8. 2020

Dylan Scudder, *Conflict Minerals in the Democratic Republic of Congo: Part of the Pentalemma Series on Managing Global Dilemmas.* ISBN 978-1-4331-7561-9. 2020

Dylan Scudder, *Mining Conflict in the Philippines: Part of the Pentalemma Series on Managing Global Dilemmas.* ISBN 978-1-4331-7632-6. 2020

Dylan Scudder, *Multi-Hazard Disaster in Japan: Part of the Pentalemma Series on Managing Global Dilemmas.* ISBN 978-1-4331-7530-5. 2020

Wesley A. Stroud, *Education for Liberation, Education for Dignity: The Story of St. Monica's School of Basic Learning for Women.* ISBN 978-1-4331-7911-2. 2021

Geanneti Tavares Salomon, *Fashion and Irony in «Dom Casmurro».* ISBN 978-1-78997-972-5. 2021

Zia Ul Haque Shamsi, *South Asia Needs Hybrid Peace.* ISBN 978-1-4331-9422-1. 2022

Mohammad Rafiqul Islam Talukdar, *Local Government Budgetary Autonomy: Evidence from Bangladesh.* ISBN 978-1-80079-528-0. 2022

Shai Tubali, *Cosmos and Camus: Science Fiction Film and the Absurd.* ISBN 978-1-78997-664-9. 2020

Angela Williams, *Hip Hop Harem: Women, Rap and Representation in the Middle East.* ISBN 978-1-4331-7295-3. 2020

Ivan Zhavoronkov (trans.), *The Socio-Cultural and Philosophical Origins of Science* by Anatoly Nazirov. ISBN 978-1-4331-7228-1. 2020

www.ingramcontent.com/pod-product-compliance
Lightning Source LLC
Chambersburg PA
CBHW060347100426
42812CB00003B/1156